Alter Ego

Poetry for the Hidden Self

Alter Ego

Poetry for the Hidden Self

Levi Johnson

Dedicated to Lindsey J. Johnson
My daughter and most poetic critic

Contents

Preface

THE ALTER EGO

The word "ego" is often understood to just mean the self. But, the ego really is the negotiator between what we really desire (the id) and what society and our conscience demands (the superego). This leaves part of the individual unsatisfied due to constant compromising. Yet, gives birth to alternative desires and methods of expression called the alter ego. Much of this has been repressed by society or may be unconscious and only comes out sporadically or when triggered. Your alter ego secretly wants to openly express its true self and to be loved. Alter Ego Poetry is an attempt to give this expression its due recognition and a proper forum.

EXISTENTIALISM

I should reveal that I am an existentialist. This poetry is not about the philosophy itself, but is about our reactions to living it. Non-fiction verse is existential since it's meaning is in the experiences of human life. If you are new to this philosophy, here is a brief summary.

Existentialism is a broadly defined philosophy based on the basic principles of the human condition. It began in the mid 1800 with Soren Kierkegaard's

concept of individual meaning in life. That is, we are responsible for creating our own meaning in life, not society or the church. In this perspective, your existence is the center of the universe. This is the opposite of determinism where external forces determine your goals and purpose.

This brought rise to John Paul Sartre famous quote "existence precedes essence." This is from his work *Being and Nothingness* (1943) that many of us read in college. Essence roughly means purpose. When a cup is made, its purpose is determined before its existence. As humans, our existence precedes our purpose.

It may sound scary being born without purpose or meaning. But, it's an open road of freedom, a key concept. You choose your own purpose, not your

—

genes. You have the freedom to define yourself. It's known as "authenticity" or acting as oneself in a self-determined manner.

Meaninglessness and absurdity exist outside of us. That is, the only meaning that exists is what we assign it. The rest of the world is meaningless without us, so it's absurd. A planet without inhabitants has no meaning
until those who can think create it. This may remind you of Rene Descartes' famous quote "I think, therefore I am." Where questioning one's own existence is proof thereof.

Anxiety or anguish is recognized as our personal response to being "on our own" in this world. The existence of a supreme being is not relevant and cannot relieve anxiety.

Anxiety is resolved by living an authentic life of purpose and meaning par your definition. Each person's experience is distinctly unique that logic doesn't need to explain.

Why is existentialism popular? Well, for me it's the sense of freedom to establish your purpose and meaning within your corner of the world. No one tells me how to think or who to be except myself—so its safe to let my alter ego out to play.

Chapter One: Slices of Life

*Slices of Life are epigrams or short verses based on
unusual situations of rambling and unique realities.
I'm beginning with short slices due to our curt
attention span from the computer aging of our minds.*

I

You KNOW the future
The footsteps are loud and clear
You're just not listening

II

A mesmerizing melody
On the wings of the moon
Awakens my idle visions
Inverts my future intent
Seduces my body to break
Into particles of sound

III

The traits of a therapist
Marble within each patient's history
Reflecting perceptions and paces
Reacting on impulse and mystery
Forever altering spaces

IV

If you sculpt beyond the self
Terse transitions, ample ambitions

If you think outside the box
Daring dreams, exciting extremes

If you're aware of all dimensions
Timeless travel, universe unravels

V

Fetish freedoms, creative emotions
Future sculpting, social change
Clever children, novel notions
Peaceful love, idea exchange

Social Darwinism

VI

I hear that tender is a time
Of sweet unconditional love
I hear whispers on the wind
From my daughter up above

I see her memory of beauty
Visions soothing my heartbeat
I see that life is a design
And creativity a window seat

VII

Time is a method of moths
    Childhood is moths of memory

Love is a curative passage
    Marriage is a passage marquee

Idealist debate contrived culture
    But, affairs are life's degrees

VIII

Teasing textures of humanity
Where machines are anatomy of art
And computers are mentors of minds
We're digitally obsolete
Breathing between heartbeats

Postmodernism

Beauty of Imbalance

Burning Man
Scorched by heat, carved by wind
Creative cultures of artistic abandon
Seeking nirvana's timeline

To clip the strings of constraint
And evolve the social swagger
You blossom in the beauty of imbalance
Burning Man

IX

Have you ever drudged for demons
Or conformed beyond the pale?
Ever lived inside a boss's thrive
Or costumed under a veil?
Have you ignored dire feelings
 Just to earn the right to exhale?
 I have

X

Each day I awake
Into profound confusion
It's all a meandering mystery
Of what to do or where to go
What to say or how to be
Of who and why I am
Everyday is a clone
Help

XI

Ideology is the oligarch of   sound
In the social commentary of   lyrics
In the rebellious outrage of   fashion
In thoughtful trespasses of   protest
In the naked expressions of   euphoria

Ideology

XII

If freedom is liquidity of mind
And meaning a paradox predicted
Does purpose have consciousness?
For an existence yet scripted?

XIII

Lascivious kisses absorb my lips
Ignited illusions sway my hips

Hungry hormones tickle me tender
I bathe myself in vicarious splendor

I lust for imaginary tremors of
An earthquake of romantic love

XIV

Grateful Dead at the helm
Wild Turkey in the park
An anthem autumn day
Of composers and opposers
Of abstracts and resisters
Until the turkey ate my mind
Gobble gobble

The Café

Smiles and memories reign
To covet the heart's café
Nostalgia restores my design
As heaven's castaway

My sentimental boutique
Like falling without a floor
And dancing between the rain
Of the closing doors

XV

To be inspired
Not by fear, but by desire
To look inside your backbone
To be lifted beyond all priors
To alter a pending existence
To be inspired

XVI

Today I'm falling fray
Yielding to memory's time
Legs linger in the mire of miles
Ailing arms are strings of vine

From a youthful carve of art
To puzzling pieces of clay
Aging imparts my wear
Today I'm fall   f

i   r

n   a

g   y

XVII

When thoughts are society's animation
And movement is patterns of mimics
When identity is a loan to the herd
Your morality is guided by sound
While insight is waiting for vision
The great divide

XVIII

Cagey campaigns, tides of temptation
Shadow seductions, cycles of cures
Rolling romances, velvet vocations
Power positions are all the contours

XIX

A quaint town in France
       Wooden shoes are carved
Until machines antiqued people
       Who threw the sabots as barrage
Now we term the squirm
       The sage of sabotage

XX

We can't escape our egos
Into the balance of instinctual demands

We can't escape intense desire
Into the grace of social commands

We can't escape the gravity of guilt
Into the integrity that washes your hands

Love

Temptations of your touch
Redesigns my path of mind
The luxury of your lips
Harmony of heavenly chimes
The ecstasy of your eyes
Evolves my edges of time

To the maestros of lingering love
And the melting of yin into yang
From the contrasts of the combined
To the hormonal range of minds

Love is always seen from behind

XXI

From first engages to paradise places
Soulful eyes to long embraces
Burgundy wine to nursery rhymes
Of heaven sent to destiny's time

Your child

XXII

To imagine
To think the unthinkable
Achieve the most remarkable
To extend the icon of greatness
Watch others build your statue
To revel a lasting legacy
Be loved by all walks
To imagine

XXIII

To mold a child, to mold a mind
To know thyself, to know what's blind

To marble traits, to marble time
To tender kinds, to leave behind

Create the direction, create the design
You are the sculptor, a genius divine

Mr. Mojo Rising

Doors open
Into the heart of Jim Morrison
Mused if he had been born
And if he is or was ever alive

To intoxicate with doubt
Turns self-defeating inside out
Perishing a pending person
To only fester and worsen
Doors closed

XXIV

To children fatherless
A gift of empty glass thought
Grow genius to what you can be
You miss not what you've sought
B E   F R E E

XXV

In the future,
you'll be a clairvoyant day dreamer
and telepathic night reader

If you're lucky

XXVI

Your LIFE REVIEW
An unconscious need for closure
An ménage of jagged meanings
Of your journey's winding road
And diamonds in the dark
To edges that evolve

Eternally

XXVII

We discover and design
We author and formulate
We love structures of cognition
That we spawn to emulate

We fashion and imagine
We compose and create
We love daydreams of ambition
And nightmares without fate

XXVIII

In the hearts of all historians
Is an empty bumbling blind man
Searching for severed synapses
For bodies of biographies
Who chisels past the riddle
For the secrets of the bold

XXIX

To the champions of ecology
An evolutionary calculus
Visions of epoch eureka
Feeling the 11th hour
Shrinking in size
so small

XXX

The genetic age
Hovering over the horizon
Terrifying the hell out of tradition
Confusing our time of existence
Leaping our spans of life
Splicing our genes
Deleting our DNA

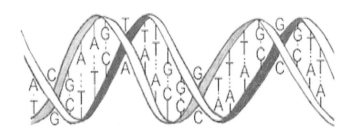

XXXI

To extend our earthly goals
Beyond the basics of survival
Is to hyper the future of cyber space
And bend the genes to speculate

Repaving your destiny's road
To clone a change unknown

Forever

XXXII

I am a drifter
I sleep under freedom's sun
Meander with intrepid moons
I sunshine with swaggers
And frown with faux pas
My solitary journey of time
Is my alter ego's flaw

XXXIII

To morning sickness, floundering flows
Of canopy clothes, destiny chose
To talking tummies, babbling babies
Of hospital hazy, God like ladies
To teasing teeth, photo sessions
Of future lessons, eternal blessings

XXXIV

"Stop, they'll put you in jail"
Froze him for a moment
Over the wall and fence
A teenage sky bound monkey
Escaping for his sanity

Asylum alumni

*When I worked in a mental hospital for children,
the teenagers were the most challenging.*

XXXV

A time to question the mind
      A mirror to rewrite the route
As vanity manages to humble
      Urgency ushers doubt
Your stage of self-reflection
      Is epiphany's empire clout

XXXVI

Enraptured by Bourbon Street
Melodies of magical history
From Jelly Roll to Fats to Louis
Ride the rhythms of soulful rhymes
Fade the fringes of frantic times

XXXVII

I partitioned my floundering peers
And blundered my primary years

I languished the depth of loves
And wrangled at work with shoves

Now I'm heaven's prey of birds
As my tears of folly rings absurd

Symphony

Renaissance's rites of reason
Bonding into culture crowns
Harmony to ears of Eden
For those who toast the town

Symphony to ears of season
Black ties and naughty gowns
Pretentious lights that beacon
Social scene of wealthy frowns

XXXVIII

Embryonic ears of a teen
An opera, symphony and ballet
A mind-opening journey so keen

My memories virtuoso of art
In concertos, sautés and librettos
Rebirths and caresses my heart

XXXIX

Do you believe in the soul?
In Gods, heaven and hell
Is your sensory supernatural
Is your meaning metaphysical
Are you reincarnated
Into a lost self
As I am?

XL

Discovery of a distant son
Thirty years removed
Hallways of hollow history
Vacuums vise the dialogue
Two passing ships at night
Just flashing our lights

XLI

To be a perfectionist
Not compulsive or obsessive
Just the calculus of a curve
Just crossed t's and dotted i's
I'm for precision of performance
That exacts onto others
Anxiety

XLII

To roll in seismic rhythms
To open harmonic gateways
Of dimensions of logarithms

A faceless frontier of infinity
Into the vacuum of the vortex
To seize the next synergy

Extraterrestrial

XLIII

Joys of an ECCENTRIC existence
Wrinkles the pages of society
From social status to personal growth
From rebellious rogue to future fate
Never harbored by the heard
Never hollow or deterred
Never searching for lost words

Free Falling

Hormonal helter-skelter
Your passage of waning libido
Schemes your gender's essence
Takes your age out for cleaning
Like free falling in a dream
Into a lightness of being

Infinity

XLIV

I counsel the elders
To renounce all attachments
To file all loves, memories and dreams
To see the end as a new beginning
To thrive in shapeless form
To envy the course
The next self

XLV

Extradition is theme
Of all bodies, minds, and souls
To taint tomorrow's dreams
I'm grounded into roots
And baked into schemes
To deny earthly pursuits

XLVI

When its time to leave the planet
We'll build some wings to ark
We'll mold a second moon
And handpick those who hark

When its time

XLVII

To testostérone and estrogen
Pendulums that love to swing
Existing between the ebb and flows
Drinking the milk love bestows

From the volumes of ego captions
To the tapestry of woven passions
The fuel of hormone enshrines
Ignites the character of designs

Your genesis

XLVIII

To dying men in prison
I can see the tears in your heart
And map the malice of your mind
I know you lost everything
All freedom, hope and time
The emptiness that pervades
Is a ghost of pantomime

XLIX

A bumpy road of fields and dreams
As vast as vision can heal itself
Blossoms on a grid of harvest plow
The ochard Ag is sterling stealth

Cycles

I am a cycle theorist
Rhythms and orbits of time
Circles of politics and people
Economies that bounce and climb

To harness these timely rotations
And genius the wane and flows
Let the patterns tempo your mind
And curate your day in chateaus

L

You're the prism of your vision
And the kaleidoscope of time
You're the parade of your particles
And the rapture of rhymes
You're the option of your oracle
And the maestro of your mind

You are sublime

LI

To warden the world of work
Like writing the same rhyme
Everyday until you scream
You're an origami paper person
That's folded all your dreams

LII

Each dawn I age a piece of myself
I gasp as it falls on the floor
I scream as it rolls down the hill
And liquefies into the shore

My parting rites of passage
Through mother earth's backdoor
Accepting my future of being
Evaporates my edges of yore

LIII

We endure a primitive world
Daily differences are danger
Fear marries hate and control
As power becomes sadistic
Politics is a paid patrol
For the narcissistic

LIV

Where social skills are battle cry
Personal deception is black tie

From machines mauling your match
To the cyber cold you catch

Digital dating is theme of esteems
For future mating test of schemes

LV

I spoke to my soul today
I told him I am ready
To make the great exchange
To fly without wings
To bond without people
To love without emotion
I am ready

Wooden Dreams

A life of competing for dreams
The strife of pursuing to scale
Your fame is a whittled horse
The heartwood of social Braille

Waive to fancy your fans
Grab the reigns, take the round
The dream of miracle moments
Is a wooden girl's playground

LVI

Diets old, diets new
Test your will, test your clout
Exalt the epoch, exalt the self
Leasing time from inside out

LVII

BARE
You are born
You accrue vast objects
Gather great knowledge
Amass wonderful friends
Reproduce the awesome
Then you die
BARE

LVIII

When parents reject you
Confidence is forever spent
Purpose is defined as pride
Love is a leveraged intent
Success is fantasy to stride

As peace of mind invents

LIX

Stretching the siblings
Into elastic personalities
Extroverting the introverts
From involuntary idleness
Redirecting lost trajectories
Into the light of identity

LX

I tilt the truth
Contrive my caring
Seduce to be smart
Pretend to be sharing
I mislead and deceive
Just to be daring

LXI

Fatherhood
Reshapes your solo shell
Takes your heart out for cleaning
Awakens a hidden purpose
To rise above all meaning

Indefinitely

Inner Child

Have you met your inner child
To find your vital voice as styled?

Freely dancing in hidden desires
The rooted cause of character fires

I'm that youthful whisper in your ear
That you ignored all through the years

The subconscious traits that still exist
Despite denial and bucket lists

LXII

Feminine fame for handsome hearts
Spun from an ancestral genius
A rare and healing tapestry
Of unconditional love
Where only mortals
Do us part

LXIII

To
die
and return
Gift or curse
A wake up call
A change of heart
A spiritual relationship
For a week

LXIV

Where do we look
For ambition and virtue
Work is a scheme of survival
Love is the path of churning
Family is the caption for culture
The alter ego still yearning
Endlessly

LXV

The whispers of bygone beings
Benevolent to future believing

I walk with shadows arm and arm
Their conversations I still charm

Relationships lost in space and time
Hearts you know are yours assigned

To conflicted souls I am a knight
For final weaves of earthly plights

LXVI

Swinging in the light of the moon
Bathing in brightness of freedom
Romancing your solo swoon

To fancy and drama your fashion
From lavishing your lure with love
To harbor your ports of passion

Cocooning

Daughter

Love is a high wire daughter
Balance is her birthright to extol
With a similarity of difference
We pagan this puzzle whole

To the whimsy of a wandering child
On the breeze of wisdom's design
To the enshrining hearts of two
And the heaven time assigns

Love

LXVII

How can I so painfully pine
For a daughter so eager elusive
I fashioned freedom in her mind
And rogue rebellion in her heart
Now empty is my chime
But, hearty is my tart

LXVIII

A slippery grip on the wind
Stealing my breath away
Galloping into the black
Until the eye of the cyclone
My moving pivot point
Spits me to the ground
Bareback

LXIX

Heat, snow, floods
Climates hungry for change
There is no refuge from pain

No substitute for fact and reason
The geysers are feeding skeptics
Cuisine of crow for their treason

LXX

Wisdom is a mood of reflection
Divine is the future of your past
To carve a unique direction
Let themes of your history's contrast

Karma

LXXI

The desperation of a circus clown
To be a fire eating, stilt walking,
Knife throwing, trapeze acrobat
A risk taker's minute of fame
For a nomad without a name

LXXII

Fermenting friends of age
Not of body, but of mind
Wrinkles of a fading future
And terror of feeble times
Withdrawing into their wombs
The nursery tomb of rhymes

Retirement

Alienation

What if I were alien?
Would you care, would it matter?
I'll bathe you in a tinted light
To mind-read you like a book
I'll enhance floundering females
To far exceed outlook
Would you care?

Would it matter?

LXXIII

Genetically gentrified
Hierarchy of débutants
Prisoners of the pampered
Idolize fathers of the fable
Worship mothers of the mask
Predetermined is your posture
Tradition is your task

LXXIV

Beauty to the beholders
To the angles and prisms of curves

Jubilance to the jesters
To the incognito and humor that serves

Vanity to the visionaries
To the foresight and dreams of nerves

LXXV

I despise pretentious parents
Who are selfish, digital or fake
Who are ghost of their cell phones
View offspring as just namesake
Who converge just to conspire
As their children will soon forsake

Irony

LXXVI

New Orleans necropolis
Masculine mausoleums mumble
They hover above the haunches
Mummies styled of stone
Fashions of the father
Timeless on their throne

LXXXII

From lovely laughter to silent strife
To the teeth and claw of lusty life

From highs and lows of roller coasters
To explosive jokers, character closures

From octane rushing through my veins
To the bipolar pilot of my plane

I fly

LXXXIII

To be a tourist is a spy
Peeking into windows eye
Taking greed in cultures air
Pilfer for their monty share
Shadow secrets are the glow
To interlopers in the know

Flower Child

Our land of vintage minds
French roast and panhandling
Prisms of tie-dye and bell-bottoms
Open ideas and harmony hearts
When peace and love rhymed
In Haight Ashbury times

Flower children and eager eyes
Benevolent hearts in hippie disguise
Future clamoring and cult exchange
In this 1960s time of change

Peace

LXXXIV

Reincarnate me out
The prisoner is shackled
With a mind of ancestral debris
Into the infinity of embodied epochs

So clever this recurring cycle
Mazes of worry, pain and mistakes
To repeat what is never finished
And finish what is never completed

Reincarnate me out

LXXXV

The allure of revolving lovers
Like playing a banjo in the rain
And hiding inside the outbound train
Sweet needles of a cactus flower
Barb the lips in the final hour

LXXXVI

Barbarically fed only once a day
Until I was baring all bones
Deceived from strokes of a doctor
Despite my constant bemoans
My mind has turned to putty
And my body to sandstone
In my cell

High Society

The adolescence of Mary Jane
New sprouts of changing times
The sheep have wooly power
To expand their narrow minds
Now thoughts are tart and tangled
While memory is redesigned

Colors melt into human hues
And dance to entertain my eyes
Sound has moved under my skin
And flows from head to sky
Marijuana is my only friend
While reality goes awry

LXXXVII

To be gay in a gray world
A social chime fear begrimes
Hiding as crooks in crannies
The Sisyphus of scathing times

LXXXVIII

Joys of San Francisco and New York
To the romance of London and Paris
From a summer's day of cafés
To steamy nights of dancing
I love urban prancing

Unhinged

LXXXIX

Romances that climb society
Are the weather of cloudy schemes
From aversion of status anxiety
To irony of conformist extremes

XC

Wyatt Earp's designer digs
Horton Hotel, Gaslamp District
Legend of a lucky lawman
Male madam to a bustling brothel
Gifted gambler game to challenge
Hero of the time (1848-1929)

XCI

The simplicity of a smile
Blossoms of the human tree
The harmony of laughter
Music of the hearts of glee
The comfort of a caress
Tender takes of thou to thee

XCII

I know not the name of my neighbors
And dream for a warm sea of strangers

Being unique is a fish without fins
Like a tear in a swamp of hot springs

To float with others who stay unknown
Just phantom comfort of nearby bones

City dwellers

Together

If you are the first to go
I'll hold your hand
And tell you it's okay

If I am the first to go
The beauty of your grace
Is my parting gift

If we go together
Our love never breaks
Through the END OF TIME

XCIII

Agenda of patriarchy
Bully those passive or smart
Man's primitive hierarchy
A leaking hole in his heart

Barbarian fear is darkness
Paranoia is keen to flee
From chains of human starkness
To dreams of being free

XCIV

Movement is time through space
Space is a movement of time
Time is the pace of movement
A continuous paradigm

XCV

Instincts of play are freedoms of clay
Confidence and mastery seek elusive prey

For the sport of mimics we compete
To the pride of victorious hearts we beat

We are the culture of social ambition
Minting our minds to rogue competition

Capitalism

XCVI

Motley motels hotly digested
Take out food barely effective
Childhood memories yelling loud
Even school was disavowed
But, I grew wings to cuddle clouds

XCVII

The twisted twenties
A slippery stage of temptations
That tampers the themes of the heart
When dreams out weigh the mind
And alter egos are still blind

XCVIII

If men lead lives of quiet desperation
Women lead lives of talkative socialization
Animals lead lives of symbolic interpretation
Insects lead lives of waste fertilization
The only important question, how you live your life

*In memory of Henry David Thoreau who championed the
freedom of human rights over governmental control.*

Voices

Seduced by the mask on the wall
Monologues directing my plight
That knots the arms of my mind

Telegraphing my every thought
Entangling each trait behind
Spiting my identity with voices
To forsake my characters entwined

Schizophrenia

XCIX

Every wrinkle you can trace
A depth of story not so subtle
Forever engraved upon your face
Your public map of private puzzles
To unmask

C

All day at the race track
Sugary sodas, fatty dogs
Habitual hearts, senility smarts
Frightened faces, growling paces
Cacophony of animal souls

CI

His failed integrity now flees
Leaving young mouths to plea

Of his own genes and dreams
Watching him twist and scheme

Now he's a glorious escapee
To curiously hover carefree

CII

From your hidden town of texting
To the de-evolution you're vexing

Your social geometry of angles
Is youth's mentality that mangles

Your voyage of notoriety is veiled
From heartbeats of society we hail

CIII

Inventive strokes of the surrealist
Must shatter all horizons beyond
To abstract the absurd, quake the queer
Engender the extreme, beget the bizarre
Everyday

CIV

When savvy struts it age, work becomes cliché
Labor of love that doubts bleeds beyond the day

Carve your wit and passion from above
Solo is your legacy and language of love

Fragments

Do you ever feel fragmented?
Ever evolve into a borrowed being
Are you hiding from a broken soul
With visions of marginal meaning

Do you lose your place in time?
Does memory fade and mumble
Can you puzzle these anxious pieces
Or does age dictate your crumble

CV

A menu mosaic of creative accrues
Music and stage are enticed pursues

Neon lights blind society's insight
City identities are copies in flight

Reflecting replicas of finicky fearers
To masquerade in a city of mirrors

Incognito

CVI

Is love the flip side of hate
And depression the jockey of joy?
Do opposite personalities attract
Is marriage a feminine ploy?
Are children the cagey extract
To copy, engage and convoy?

CVII

Running without feet
        On the rush of rambling wind
Thinking without intent
        On the instincts of ancestral kin
Existing without anatomy
        On my soul's task within

CVIII

The greatest mind of modern times
Birthed the radio's heavenly chimes

Bestowed earth's electricity free to all
Yet, jealousy sabotaged his protocol

So threatened were the dim witted
The genius FEAR never permitted

Tesla (1856-1943)

CIX

Flaunting fashions, ego passions
Delirious designs, beacon shines
Cultural currency, wealth security
Jewelry gems, joyful femmes
Status tingles the bliss of mingles

CX

Racism is back in style
The President clued the clones
Where hate and fear is all the rage
To bounce on rubber backbones

Fab Four

Sgt. Pepper's Lonely Hearts Club Band
Icon of the idiom and hope for wings
Music of a time that propels beyond
The world's ground swell to foretell

Changing the culture of the century
With harmony and lyrics pristine
In an era of elevated idols
And emptiness looking to belong

Frames of Identity

CXI

Unbeknown to me
I appended an alcoholic
Who loudly laughs and parties
Yet stifles his sobriety of sound
To design his destiny
To persuade his past
To be whole

CXII

How quickly does love perish?
I savor the touch of steamy kisses
And favor the wealth of emotional riches
Yet, you miss not relationships awry
When baby girl is your lullaby

CXIII

Period plantations shape tourist travel
Stirring the ghosts of fear and gravel

A gallery of slavery parts so savage
A history of victim hearts in ravage

Brutal ideology of cynical cults
Archaic minds of incited results

*I wrote this after a tour of the plantations
with slave quarters in the southern United States.*

CXIV

Norbert Yancey
San Francisco street gentry
Of lyrics and melody and rhyme
Fifty years of tourist envy
To legacy heaven's pastime
(1935-   )

CXV

B R E A K   F R E E
of pompous people
partisan politics
social shaming
status seekers
B R E A K   F R E E
of old insecurities
idle identities
liquor lunatics
lifelong labor
B R E A K   F R E E

CXVI

Married to the matrix of money
Where sweat and tears are woven
Into a fabric without heart
Too daunting to divorce
Peeking through the bars
Toiling in the dark

Seashore

Endless journey of golden beaches
Sultry surfers waxing the waves
Glistening sun seducing your skin
Buried toes in sandy caves
The fluty sound of a violin

Salty breeze cleaning your mind
Sun worshipers and moon dancers
Who rebirth and rejoice in the blue
Vast liquid of our species
Our opium of déja vu

CXVII

Children playing in fantasy
Nuances of a yearning nostalgia
Hiding in the caverns of time
A wandering inner child
Banging the walls of the womb
Realizing I am yet to be born

CXVIII

The virtuosos of eons past
Breathing ancestral wisdom
Yet, we live in numb repetition
In the small of minted minds
A stunted species of habits
Evolve the grace of decline

CXIX

Yachting in the bay of arks
With fluid bodies of bounty
Escapism swims with sharks
In the velvet of zealot county

CXX

The envy of escaped embraces
The passage of people and places

Slithering through my fingers
Triggers a frenzy fate lingers

To be the face of flowing time
Exalts the pace of an open mind

CXXI

Very odd identities
I carousel the crazy
Or simply the misfit ones
Littered with archaic labels
Sautéed by secret societies
Protects the fearful from themselves
In a world of elves

CXXII

Harmony is the hope of humanity
Integrity is the canopy of character
From archetypes of ancestral oaks
To unconscious trait evokes
We rise

Age

Can you see past my wrinkles?
Into the playful heart of a child
Can you see my angles still mingle?
From the biography of all the smiles

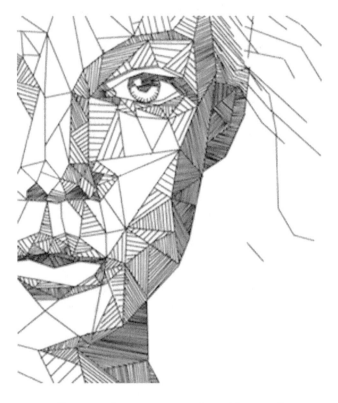

Can you lose your youth and beauty?
From the ecstasy of time
Can you give your personality?
To a soul's paradigm

CXXIII

To know thyself is to know thy future
The meaning of your benchmarks
Hark your heart and mute your mind
To envy this mystery to embark

CXXIV

Sami Sunchild
The Red Victorian angel
Herald heart of Summer of Love
Historic hotel of peace and art
Sculpting the culture like Descartes
(1925-2013)

CXXV

To passing thresholds of people
I see silhouettes of the final dance
Measuring the space remaining
And the passage of rites to chance

Graduation

CXXVI

Your season of second acts
Spellbound with contemplation
Mystified by captured occasion

Urgency is your umpire
To extend the expiring edges
And stretch your space of mind
To the space of time

CXXVII

To embrace the existential self
Is an internal battle of integrity
From historical traits of awareness
Into your crystal ball of purpose
For expressions of archetypes
Your evolutionary verses

CXXVIII

Roger Bannister
First miler to fleet under four
Not his most famous talent
Skills of neurology his core
To legacy his love so gallant
(1929 to 2018)

Losing Time

When the present paces the past
Your balance beckons to beware

When the backbone begins to bow
Your stage is degrees to prepare

When friends are dazed and dangled
Your fate in the future is dared

When this tempo thins your space
You finalize your epic affair

If you have time

CXXIX

When you reject the sheep of society,
expect to be called odd, rogue, eccentric,
deviant, and even crazy—music to my years

An identity frontier

CXXX

Humming harlots
Rhythms to the beat of the street
Who must mezzo their motives
Harboring the treat of discrete
Who must blossom human flaws
Hiding in the heat of the sweet
Humming harlots

CXXXI

Gothic spires of the Catholic proud
Standing silent in the glory of times
Speaking loud to those on clouds
A blessing of heavenly chimes

Notre Dame

CXXXII

Winding walks and twisted talks
Chinatown to fishing docks

I pine for Sundays in the City
Nostalgic bonding stalls self-pity

I compass my culture and domain
Chain of time is not in vain

CXXXIII

To the clockwork rhythms of man
Seducing our moods by tempos
Messaging our bodies with beats
Shaping our thoughts into moments
Challenging the observing ego
To rebel

CXXXIV

Sorority sisters
Odyssey of shifting sands
Where social status can disguise
Personalities with hidden hands
A curious culture to ritualize
And a passport to a foreign land

Mirrors

Are your memories subject to age
And thoughts tangled themes?
Do mirrors maul your image
Of kisses, places and dreams?
Does time's erosion alter
Your history of joyful esteems?

Be thankful for a wrinkled mirror
If you crinkled here at all
If passion engaged your edges
And meaning expanded your mind
If you danced and shared your dreams
Be thankful for the time

CXXXV

I stretch my fingers around
The dawn of a lost mentality
I swim in a rogue romance
And the age of a new reality

My heart does not dissolve
My mind does not dismiss
My only sense of identity
Is my lover's French kiss

The hidden self

CXXXVI

Cigarettes cage my fuming friend
Whiskey numbs his mind to mend

Caffeine coaxes his body a chance
Cocaine hoaxes his virtual romance

Society's crutches are all acclaimed
Are walking coals till all aflame

*This is dedicated to my friend who became
addicted to cocaine.*

CXXXVII

To the cutting edge, cultural change
Winds of desire are benefit exchange

To balance romance, a pump so primed
Children and family are futures of rhymes

To social service, hands without gloves
To savor our hearts in a summer of loves

CXXXVIII

Mediocrity is the air we breath
Morality has slipped underground
Virtue weeps for political vandals
Veiled by a smirk and a frown

Integrity is a lost identity
Humanity is a closed playground
From charlatans who starve society
To the cannibals who eat the town

Our leaders

CXXXIX

Group identities are a loss of self,
Self-identity is a loss of group,
Gene expression is the only true identity

The Rain of Life

She stands
with roses for eyes
and roots wrapped around her ankles
she counts every time I see her cry
except she does not drown in the rain

She is reborn
and she is not scorched by the fire
it only matches her heart
and if she is
she emerges from the ashes

I guess I never saw someone
cry so beautifully

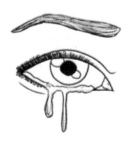 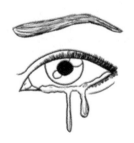

© Lindsey Johnson

Chapter Two: Unpredictable Love

Your alter ego wants to be loved. But, we all know how unpredictable the maze of romantic love can be. Yet, we are intensely drawn into its belly time after time. Creating a cycle that often fails to mature leaving us longing and confused. Some people spend their lives seeking a bond that is never found. This is the most intense existential experience in our lives. Join me on this journey of emotional twists and turns.

Our ability to perceive and act upon our limitations will transcend all aspects of the heart.

To the love of unpredictable content

Google Eyes

Streams and streams of goggle eyes
Flowing through the sultry skies

Steamy nights of fantasy's quest
When the moonlight is your gauge
Dripping from throbbing breasts
Your body has come of age

When love flow is a fountain
Your mind has liquefied
Each breath conquers each mountain
With streams of goggle eyes

When youth is the spring of urge
You're the heaven that I haunt
Our hearts and minds to merge
Sweet lips are all I want

Streams and streams of goggle eyes
Flowing through the sultry skies

*This was my first lyric poem that was converted
to a song and became recorded.*

Light Kisses

Light kisses are precious prisms
    Of the light that love embeds
    Of the light reserved for a child
    And the light desire misled

My lips are a rhythmic rogue
    That drinks the elixir of my mind
    Juggling my better judgment
    Rendering my insights blind

Wedding bells, a chorus of capers
    Lessons of the journey precede
    But, kisses impostor me impulsive
    And campaigns me to concede

The ecstasy of envy kisses
    So silky and sweet and steeped
    Unhinges me into excesses
    Where fantasy never sleeps

Secret Sweetheart

To secret loves, to saucy Suzanne
Of amorous arms, of arms of life spans

To self redemptions, to rendezvous
Of past relations, past misconstrues

To femininity, to fantasy thereof
Of uncanny contours, of energy of love

To a golden mane, to liquid blue eyes
Of gingerbread gifts, of salacious surprise

To dreams of two, to be campaigns
Of characters on course, of course champagne

To inebriate we, to be the inevitable
Of paradox dare, of paradox pleasurable

To residing with men, to men of garnish
Of tempting fate, of tears of tarnish

To her daring capture, the house of hormones
Of me screaming rapture, of reckless condones

She swaggers in the face of teardrops.

Chisel My Heart

I pose forlorn be-   side myself like
a statue of cold stone.   I treat my heart as an
elf, elusive and unknown. I forever dream to view
when a sculptor chisels my heart. Who configures
it into two and defines our love fine art. I wait
for darkness to prism and for the dawn
to discern. I breathe vague
optimism of eternal
doubt and
yearn

Vexing Vibrations

Lonely people falling into love grids
Vision drinks the tears that curiosity forgives

Hinders of hope to merging the minds
Yet, habits of hearts are webbing the blind

Contours of love are innocence and Broadway
Lures of high marquee and novel naiveté

Opening the heart to collecting flirtations
Is tempting the traits of vexing vibrations

Characters of the Night

To uncover the cupid of night
I creep between the chill
Leaping over the edges
A chameleon from before
Translucence is my breeze
Drafting through her door

Caressed by nervousness
Untangled by the warmth
Words of altered meanings
Confusions to explore
Now fractures into pieces
In mind fields of her floor

To fancy moulds of clay
Wit and heart reshaped
To a fate without form
From rascals of rapport
To the tingle of tainted love
My character will deplore

*This is in memory of my college relationship when I was
19 years old and she was 34. You experiment when young
before the superego of judgments limits your scope.*

Pending Hearts Clown

Dawn of rhyming feelings
Ruffles a scuffled sound
Awakens a willful being
Pending hearts new clown

He delights me into laugher
Or ignores me till I cry
A tease of southern comfort
Or kisses from the sky

His balance is your trapeze
Testing the intrepid and sincere
In a stratosphere conceived
Where lonely hearts cohere

Gamble of matching traits
The fulcrum of forecast
Triggered by the historical
Parental patterns recast

Comedian with your virtues
Can't reverse your kin
Dance of personalities
Ignorance is a sin

Care taking is the magic
Concerto of your time
Tolerance is the joker
Success is sublime

Love in Sync

Love is a kilowatts kiss
On my lascivious lips
Wet currents of tenderness
Rendering me eclipsed

Love is empathic elixir
On an island of paradise
Harmony is the mixture
Two hearts beat precise

Love is a sensuous touch
A silky smooth embrace
Your skin to relish the fuss
A hypnotic herb of grace

Love is ecstasy's mind
The genius of congealing
Hidden traits combined
Blossom fugitive feelings

Love is a decoding devotion
You bestow yourself beyond
The intensity of this motion
Is the backbone of your bond

Love is a clairvoyant moment
Anticipating lips in sync
Compromise is so potent
Salvation is your mink

Love Stages

When touch is electric
Endorphins are king
My heart is bouncing
Hormones on a spring

Arouse body and mind
Intoxicate and stun
Self-esteem explodes
I melt in stage one

Age of trait discovery
Patterns of the past
To weigh and to muse
Your fabled forecast

Caring and awareness
Cement the character glue
Insight and empathy
I coalesce in stage two

If we can only temper
Each other's personal flaws
Kinship of a lifetime
Dances with ego applause

Sculpt the romantic rhyme
Strut the social marquee
Genius your epic time
I hunger for stage three

*The fact that love has stages often baffles and defeats
many. Most relationships break up after the passion ends
and never reach the settling in stage.*

Passion Scares

I dearly miss my romantic mend
The structure of my heart is lost
My sense of self cannot transcend
Love's winter is a blanket frost

I bury the emptiness within myself
In shadows of outwitted acquiesce
Breached by phonies who coup as elves
Agony defines how rogues finesse

Now I'm an island in a sea so cold
Bypassed by boats and barge
I fear my heart was left to mould
Paralyzed by passion scares

Untie The Knot

Desperate tears of society
Emotional stage directives
Folkways to anxiety

Culture's crumbling hope
Built on sharp legal razors
Lovers slippery slope

Follow the sheepish script
Mindless as a mimic
Until dissolves to crypt

Tied the knot I dared
Rites of passage feared
Peeled the dread as shared

Intolerance is the wedge
Coupling fuels the spirit
Don't get cut on the edge

Secret of amour to dare
Cohabit only with diamonds
Rock flames melt razor affairs

Heart or Mind

Overlook not the heart, house of feelings,
    birthplace of love, sanctuary of caring

Overlook not the mind, keeper of meaning,
    coach of reason, schoolroom of life

Favor the heart, be involved, but dependent,
    favor the mind, be single, but accomplished

Minding the heart, is mending the mind,
    of heartless minds of love

Questions d'Amour

Do you crave a real relationship
Not revolving door affairs?
Do you optic your heart for love
Rather than collections of fanfare?

Do you believe in soul mates
Rather than evolve into self-aware?
Do you strive for compatibility
Rather than personality dares?

Do you yearn for true sincerity
Not the pretentious words of sass?
Do you love beyond the self
Rather than cast your ego in glass?

Computer Dating

Are you ready for
the bounce of rubber hearts
of a machine driven courtship
in a matrix of slippery smarts?

Are you ready to
undress your seeking soul
into a risk of erotic emotions
while dangling in a public role?

Are you ready to
rank your traits like a wine
matching motions that parallel
a mirror misaligned?

Are you ready to
invent your ideal intentions
with passages of pseudo perfections
breathless for a minor reflection?

Are you ready to
meet with expectations galore
and dance with the incognitos
just to fall and bounce on amour?

*If you ever experienced online dating, then you're aware
of the pseudo and incognito aspects. Yet, it is possible to
find a partner if you see through the smoke and mirrors.*

League of Loves

If my heart had any innings
I'd have a league of loves
Anticipation is grinning
Until I take off the gloves

First inning thrown in college
Idealistic and immature
A stormy sense of knowledge
A whirlwind to endure

An early marriage was my teacher
In the classroom of the heart
Where love was the preacher
In the chapel a la carte

Four years to melt the mirage
The tuition of hindsight
In scripting the next corsage
I parlay as playwright

Next twenty two years is a song
A beautiful daughter to tout
Preserved by nothing wrong
Destroyed by simple doubt

Latent pitchers still cohere
Love stages will transcend
One more spin in the sphere
To my league of lovely mends

Curve of Heaven

Solo flight of being
Hopeful future dreaming
Youthful selfish leanings

Naked upon life's rock
Acute awareness of emptiness
A passionless drifting clock

Instinct's organic aspiration
Epiphany of pedigree
Exalt the next generation

Miraculous child unfolds
Gifting precocious flair
A miracle to future mould

Fringes of soul are reached
Contour of love explodes
To adore and heal and teach

Keener morph of meaning
Eternal hearts of harmony
Fused together, dance forever

Father esteemed identity
Curve of earthly heaven
Defining dauntless destiny

*The transition from being single to fatherhood is like
climbing out of the snow into the beat of a warm heart.*

Romantic Friends

I'm your morsel in the morning
I'm the carnival on your cake
I'm the triumph on your toast
And the sizzle in your steak

You're a saint in my sandwich
You're the tango in my tea
You're the lavish on my lips
And the lock to my key

I'm the fantasy in your flame
I'm the eager in your eyes
I'm the maestro of your movement
And the cringe when you cry

You're the thrill in my touch
You're the swagger in my smart
You're the tailor of my thoughts
And the harness of my heart

Running for Romance

Her flowing mane is long and lingers
With amber and crimson highlights
Intoxicating eyes of hazel heaven
Little seas of my fantasy's delight

Lean legs of muscle and strength
Tenaciously trotting the track
Hypnotized by majestic motions
Taking toll of my heart's feedback

Forty laps of dashing dialogue
A concert of toiling teamwork
I swagger to swoons of love
While chatting my body berserk

She's my perfect equal of passion
The one I'm secretly seeking
I'll abandon the identity I own
And surrender my satin speaking

Plans for a paradise pending
A split second on the freeway
My shattered heart to paltry pieces
Heaven breathes a breath away

My love interest was a young attorney who was killed in
an auto accident at the age of 31 leaving a lasting mark on
my heart.

Little Feet

A little foot asleep in my hand
Not quite the length of a finger
Velvety smooth, soft and warm
For hours and hours I linger

The frail of a nightingale
She lies on a bed of white
The hospital maternity ward
To thread the needle of light

To envy and bestow creation
To enhance and alter identity
I remix, reshape and recast
New edges of ego agility

To widen the heavens of my heart
And narrow the maps of my mind
A little girl is given to me
To vault my frame of time

In the tapestry of a woven future
In the wonder of pride and esteems
To what the future can caper
Into a father to child's dreams

*After my daughter was first born, the hospital
kept her overnight for respiratory problems.
I'll always cherish that evening of bonding
through her little foot while watching over her.*

Clockwise

Why is romantic love so fleeting?
Beauty blossoms a year or two
Regardless of length or marriage
Hormones of ecstasy adieu

Wisdom seeks not a lover
A comparable mind instead
Relationships are but an alliance
That endures beyond misled

Is this a falling out of love
Or falling into friendship
Is it the course of the universe
Or the irony of courtship

So I pick my heart up off the floor
With the savvy to yet revise
These revolving doors to open again
In the time of new clockwise

Chapter Three: Psychology in Poetry

When you're a psychotherapist for 36 years, you are
privy to unusual and interesting human deviations.
Yes, it can be gut wrenching and even scary at times.
Especially when I worked in the state penitentiary
mental health dept. for many years. Going to therapy
is just the alter ego asking for a little nurturing with
an open mind.

The psychology of poetry is a catharsis of hidden
feelings into the infinite curiosity of seeking voyeurs.

x

96

Content is to psychology
as instincts are to behavior

I am Therapist

I am the second edge of a neurotic wedge
for which they feel so numb.
I am the squirm of all their memory worms
sprinting to outrun.
I am the squeaky sigh of unhinging minds
turned over and outdone.

I am a magic wand of a mystery beyond
free spirit that marquees.
I am the time traveler finding cracks in hell
for glorious escapees.
I am the hired hand made of shifting sand
messaging the bourgeoisie.

I am your flirtation looking for salvation
basking in the night.
I am the pulsing waves of your hollow caves
mossed with hindsight.
I am everyday and you are sponge of clay
absorbing new insights.

Edges of Broken Faces

Smile floats a greeting
Rare boat in these parts
Arranged is our meeting
Before insight imparts

Capitalism was his fame
Now dangling to survive
Fallout with a spouse
His status now archived

Her drama is a dagger
She arrives on cue
Cries fear for her life
Engraves him in the zoo

Parole glazes him over
Roller coaster hell
Life weeps in the balance
Tears of a morsel cell

We had a little fight
My hands around her throat
I didn't kill her then
Now I'm a scapegoat

Sharp edges of broken faces
Shredding minds of time
Cleft in their paces
Eternal parting chimes

This person was doing 15 to life for attempted murder.
His wife appeared at each of his parole hearings to
successfully protest his release.

Retroactive Mind

Aptly archived in murky minds
I'm the therapist drama designs

Twisters of tears have filled my ears
Screams of souls yearning for years

When life is meandering in a maze
Pondering purpose is eyes to glaze

Memory triggers of hidden traits
Wrenching guts with faltered fates

To the tantrums of chaotic thought
And the demons of neurotic fraught

When retroactive is your mind
Your future is pending from behind

Your retroactive fabled task
Is to part with egos of the past

Or life is nothing but typecast

Psychology of Poetry

Like running naked in the woods
A playground of open thought
A melting pot of reason
Transforming what we're taught

Travel far beyond the ego
To the dark depths of the id
Caverns of the hidden
Repressions you forbid

Revamp all experiences
With the ink of a pen
Recast your own identity
And triumph over zen

Judgment is suspended
You're the therapist of the page
Romance to all emotions
Gentle love to burning rage

Your secret life review
Enlightened by willful extremes
Is exposing hidden desires
As words reshape your dreams

Instincts spark creativity
Your character's unique response
For inspired ideology
It's a bard's renaissance

Mind of Mirage

Today the sky, black with fright
  Edges of my vision, icy white
    Too wild to brave, wind and sleet
      Desolate times, savage streets

Today I'm chambered, so confined
  Edges of my body, not my mind
    Wild to amuse, fake or mistake
      Derelict dreams, caverns create

Today's fantasy, reality's fable
  Edges of sanity, swagger unstable
    Wild hallucinations, out on patrol
      Desperate to wrap, a mind's loophole

Today I obscure, prying voices
  Edges of reality, crumbled choices
    Paranoid delusions, a moving montage
      Babbling themes, a mind of mirage

Healing has Liquid Tracks

All the lovely people
Locked in broken history
Searching for the sequel
To unseal their mystery

Bearing their dismay
Pain spilling on the floor
Feelings that betray
Fester when I explore

I throw a spider's net
Tight loops for no escape
To capture their mindset
Close all the dire drapes

Life is accepting disaster
No fault of their own
Parents made of plaster
Long shadows and tombstones

Revolve into the past
Redefine memory's events
New dialogue to forecast
Conflicts are lost segments

Each week is another step
Gut wrenching to the max
Shedding the tears that slept
Healing has liquid tracks

Life Maps are Faces

Faces are life maps of hidden intent
    Uncovered are traces that we resent

A moving mask that won't conceal
    An internal buffet of privy appeal

Belated smiles are shadows in flight
    Lovely contours redesign the night

Seductive eyes calm drifting hearts
    Wrinkles that part are abstract charts

Lips mumbling words before heard
    Canvas betrays of inner songbirds

Facial emotions flash before seen
    Seduces the savvy to read your genes

Studies in psychology reveal that lips mumble true feelings
before those spoken and emotions are briefly displayed on
your visage before you react. Have you noticed?

Garden of Dreams

In my garden of heavenly dreams
I'm swinging on grape vines
Dancing on dandelions
Surfing rays of sunshine

An oasis of captured wonders
Deep and dark and bold
Nightly subconscious dramas
Schemes of shifting blindfolds

Auroras of unfolding events
I'm echo dissecting inside
To reconstruct a realism
Of images once denied

Moving symbols of meanings
Following me from confined
To potential the patterns forward
In my fractal frame of mind

I break into particles of light
In a future of personal extremes
To glimpse my next identity
In my gardens of heavenly dreams

*Freud said that dreams are the royal road to the
unconscious. Analyzing my dreams over the years gave me
a self-understanding that I wouldn't have otherwise.*

Driftwood

My vision bares people transparent
Your feelings are cagey to know
They harbor your motel of history
Where only the subconscious can go

I know why your father ignored you
And your mother had passive hands
Why lucid romances are bungled
And your friends are social quicksand

I can paint your painful past
And alter your conflicted campaign
I know your face is sculpted by fear
And how to unlock your domain

Your true character is designed
The rites of culture are captive
You're living in mirrors of mirage
To keep your thoughts distracted

Just close your eyes and follow my voice
As we journey to your inner childhood
Relive and re-task those old dialogues
And dismiss the scraps like driftwood

The Adopted Mind

A backbone of bliss until abyss
You've been resoundingly rejected
By those dearest who care the most
To provide those needs so protected

Mossy mothers throughout the world
Have sacrificed since the dawn of time
To find a way to cargo their children
Except for the one I mistaken mine

The excuse of poverty is so perilous
With age and readiness an empty glass
To those thirsty for depth of personal truth
And rationale for this blatant bypass

The custody of childhood clouds
A tsunami on memory's shore
This identity won't release my ego
As I stand on life's trap door

*Adopted children often have identity and fear of
abandonment issues. They often become over achievers
in society as a way of compensation. Steve Jobs is an
excellent example.*

The Tower

Stone face tower
Scar drawn neck
Mammoth steel shoulders
Orange jumpsuit a wreck

Weathered face of storms
Lizard skin that shines
Burning eyes intently staring
Pupils gorging mine

Distrustfully melts himself
Onto a metal chair
Iron door crashes closed
Vibrates my bones to beware

Now it's just the tower and I
Confined to a windowless cell
Dissecting for an hour
As I try to soothe his hell

The core of a hired murderer
My challenge of a lifetime
Hyper vigilant is my resolve
As I vie with verbal chime

No excuses he proclaims
I've done all that they say
Puffing his chest out
 I can't forget whom I turned grey

Congratulations I do say
You're doing insightfully well
You've integrated your behavior
And aligned it right with hell

The Depths of Diary

Deeper and deeper into the dark
Are unconscious room hallmarks
Parceled off from your main mind
Where tabooed
thoughts
confine

Hiding and hiding is idle ideal
Obscurity only the devil can heal
Self expression is yours assigned
Propelling a
malingered
mind

Memories and memories are crying
For portrayal the tears are flying
To diary pages of excited embraces
Unlock your history
of heavenly
paces

Words and words laying you bare
Agony and ecstasy are yet to beware
Protected by the privacy of your pen
Now loved by the
zeal of your
zen

Sorting Through the Spin

Confined to a rubber room
Moonlight without clothes
A blanket of yesterday's gloom
Heartbreak to yet expose

Social chaos to deplore
Remnants the cops dragged in
To begin my dissecting chore
In sorting through the spin

He moved like a caged animal
And mumbled a grisly voice
He stunk of alcohol
I gave him a dire choice

To bounce the rubber box
Clothes accrued to you
Conform to the custody clock
Respect the social stew

"I killed my best friend
I was too drunk to drive"
Death should be my mend
While pain and tears survive

Screams and cries extend
Medication and suicide watch
For healing his ego must bend
The curse of eternal botch

*When you work in a county jail, each newly arrested
inmate is to be evaluated in the morning by staff. You
never know what the cops dragged in the night before.*

The Internship

Society's pretentious shepherds
In long coats of snow leopards
Obscured from the heedful heartland
Are characters shifting in sand

Escorted into the fallen fray
A pageant of patients on display
Asylum of those languishing lost
Just skeletons from their frost

Detained in the dungeon room
Feeling estranged and entombed
On a mechanical metal bed
A stretched and shackled skinhead

My chest is bursting with pain
My eyes are burning butane
Seeking the door with my frown
"Come and help us hold him down"

Are you crazy, this man will fry
My silent screams are blinded cries
Terror's thoughts are twisted fate
"Grab his leg and use your weight"

Electrodes clamped to his head
Electric EXPLOSION of a warhead
Bouncing and thrashing like a rag doll
Through a foaming mouth of pitfalls

So is my lesson to learn and partake
I had not the strength to help or forsake
From the voltage that shocks the victims
To the bullies of the mental moth systems

Bye Polar

Nightly insomnia, a lingering blues
A magazine of mania, for me to muse

Gripping thoughts, racing the horse
Better judgments, dash to divorce

It's frantic speed, it's your heartbeat
Your social boldness, exceeds discreet

Wild self-esteem, exceeds the moon
Your urgent dream, a sexual swoon

Verbal forays, a twisting vortex
Candor bounces, like a bad check

Your every behavior, a barreling train
Your every motion, a strain of cocaine

In biochemistry, the devil's workshop
For soaring above, hysterical hilltops

To being oblivious, a conquer of strife
To being unhinged, the zest of life

My spin of utopia, to last only a week
My genetic rebels, return to meek

A spin of polarity, these frenzied fates
A parallel reality, my mind creates

Uncork the Traits

Absolute vow of head and heart
Crossroads of empathy and science
With a Hippocratic oath to impart

Caretakers sculpt unwitting
Children molded so early
To a fickle of unknown fitting

Understand and usurp the past
Arduous and wishful whimsy
Challenges your reality mask

To submerge the client's crust
And swim with trauma's turns
Sharing pain is bond of trust

Uncorking those traits yet free
Your phoenix that lives within
Restyling your rogue history

The integrity of a healing hope
Making a difference my muse
Through volatile valleys and slopes

The Tangled Therapist

Therapists are pending people
Self twisted egos of drought
Heart twisted feeling of chaos
A fraternity faux pas of doubt

Enthralled by explanations
To hybrid their hidden holes
Arming themselves with jargon
To pretense a cruise control

Content to heed your heart
And take your mind out for cleaning
While exacting a pound of flesh
 You're left to meander the meaning

The secret no one supposes
Only half can manage to mend
So buried in broken bunkers
Characters of a prior pretend

Realities of tangled therapists
Are ropes choking their core
Let your heart float with a friend
 In the beauty of a mutual mentor

Mystery of a Mender

Mental tremors, time can't temper
Old obsessions, mystery's mentor

Energy eclipses, edges of sleep
Dancing dreams, define next leap

To future ideas, seamless solutions
I am the whiskey, social revolutions

Banish the bullies, no bondage or power
To free humanity, democracy's flower

Today's regimes, these criminals plots
Quick to slay, new pivotal thoughts

Fabled freedoms, a cracked facade
Scouts of treason, an elected fraud

My tough thoughts, a soft sword
Of blind ideology, on lost hoards

To survive the flood, survive the drifts
Angle your ark, hope integrity shifts

Marriage Counseling

Salvation for the quaking
Therapy hands for eyes
Zig zaging and care-taking
The art of exposing disguise

It's all her fault
His shifty eyes claim
She won't act like a wife
Her heart is darts of flames

He refuses to mind the house
Inebriates all weekend
Squeaking like a mouse
His mentality is bookends

Stymied hearts are frostbite
From fear that over controls
And anger haunts from hindsight
That bunkers nurturing roles

Balance your analogy
Shed grandma's paradigm
Design of equal scrip
The successful path of time

Decipher quirky traits
Relationship's sticky grill
Integrity has open gates
When commitment is treadmill

Conducting marriage counseling doesn't guarantee that you'll have better relationships. You're just more aware of the many styles that can go awry. At the end of the day, it's all about compromising to work through differences.

Ageless Anxiety

Cyclones of expectations
Blood pressure to perform
Beyond obsessive fixations
Vein rapids in wave form

Stomach is scorched acid
Tricksters of the swarm
Mind is melting plastic
Sisters of the norm

Trauma is manic rubble
On exhausted neuro-pathways
Triggered by memory bubbles
Defeated, alone and dismayed

Suspense of daily doubts
Is my partnership with time
Inside are screams and shouts
A reality that never rhymes

My heart jumps my chest
Break dancing on the floor
My will is just a guest
This mentor is my war

Anxiety's core is energy
Just open motivation's door
To thrive inside this synergy
And embrace it to explore

A Note to My Soul

I am equally aware of you as you are of me
Two separate intents ambitious for immortality
Your energy photons, I feel, but can't retrieve
Our purpose, I know, is meant for us to weave

The key of hypnosis has deceived your doors
Revealing your life between lives of yours
Sphere of love and harmony unrivaled on earth
The utopia you call home until you rebirth

A time will rhyme when my mind goes blind,
And all I've done here is archived and assigned
In the heavenly library for spiritual schooling
Earthly lessons set previews for next fueling

You'll bereave the embrace of hugs and soft hands
Yet, gain orbits of freedoms and soulful life fans
I know your memory includes my traits and times
Reshaped you part hippie and designer of rhymes

*In the "Destiny of Souls" the author hypnotized more than
7000 people over a 40-year period. Clients are able to
remember their past lives and their lives between lives.
The details in this verse are from these many accounts.*

Chapter Four: Mother Nature

Mother nature is there for us from the moment we are conceived to beyond our departure. She is our only true and lasting mother for the generations of time. I never underestimate her beauty and power. This chapter begins with what I call poem pairs. This is just a result of parallel themes that compliment each other. Join me as she caresses us as a prelude to plucking out our hair.

Enlightenment is learning how to be parentally involved with mother nature.

Organically grown content

Birth of Sunrise

Dew
Drops window pane
Moisture of thought and frost
Moonlit passing clouds
Echoes of twilight
lost

Sizzling
Cup in palms
Brewing open fingers
Dissolves me into calm
Body's mood
lingers

Creamy
Luxury slippers
Poured around my being
Awakens a novel soul
Kinship of new
healing

Romance
Of mental sunrise
Hereafter slopes the day
A self-defining moment
Inspired by dawn's
ballet

Dancing Sunset

Mesmerized
By kaleidoscopic clouds
On roads of prism and wind
Symphony for crowds
Strums my heart's
violin

Inflaming
My passions in disguise
In a rolling mosaic bonfire
As multiplied by my eyes
Abstracts my body's
desire

Bones
Dripping with tension
Thoughtlessly melts away
Maze of apprehension
Elopes with another
day

Twilight
Chimes a style
Toil bouquets to play
Create a new dimension
Dance with dusk's
ballet

Spring's Design

Champagne of spring's terrain
Meadows hatching like eggs
Prism blooming domains
Rock stars with rainbow legs

Biology birthing to incite
Cubs and chicks and deer
Destiny perking to ignite
Erupting me to cohere

To awaken my annual sleep
Transported in wrinkles of time
Ecology collides and sweeps
Botanical vines to climb

To be loved by endorphins
That the thoughtful sun assigns
To have euphoria as my potion
A déja vu of spring's design

Autumn's Rhyme

My big oak tree is smiling
With seasonal rhythms of cheer
Releasing golden healing
Endearing the sun to appear

Gently floating foliage
When mingled about my head
Triggers my yearning for youth
To folic the genes inbred

Holiday feasts adhere
Cult rituals of social appeal
Familiar stories of yore
In nostalgia's orbiting reel

From crimson light to steal
To expiring time to climb
Creativity gains a bounce
In this chilly air of rhymes

Changing Seasons

Flying formations of harmony
The squawk of the geese high above
Cohorts of an urgent fraternity
Southward bound to another love

So misty and carving the breeze
Twisting the autumn leaves about
Entwines my lost seasons of time
Entangles my thoughts into doubt

Milestones of memory's moments
I watch the children grow and leave
Silent screams of fleeting seasons
Or cordial captions for all achieved

My mind is a tool for a limitless heart
Like a sculptor with his chisel
A change of time is an apple of art
And a springboard for all that crystals

I savor each sequel of the seasons
As my pivot point progresses
To digress in a direction that equals
A dimension that time transgresses

Nature's Path

A passage through a secret forest
You are the fleetness in the beauty
Passing trees like winds of chorus
Running is my sculpting duty

Racing though this space of time
To springboard youthful breeze
Joy ignites this fanatic pace
For euphoria to trapeze

Shifting anatomy of science
Is swimming in vascular lanes
When we dash through DNA
We break nature's chains

To the climate of mental clarity
And oxygen of a mind exchange
We are evolving bio entities
In a house of genetic change

From craving small mutations
To biology's grand conclusion
Running increases cell division
Nature's path of evolution

*Studies show that running increases cell proliferation
and neurogenesis. But, that's no excuse to engage with
your run as if it had consciousness.*

Sensory Sunday

Sunday has a sensory unique to its array
An off center reality designed to breakaway

For some an obligation to a higher power
While others just rejoice in a whiskey sour

Sunday exploration sets the flavor of my feet
I love to swagger along to be beat of the street

Crayons in my mind designs a freedom song
City Lights Book roar is my rhythm to belong

Savory is the flavor of fluid attitudes
To a way of thinking between the interludes

A day of steamy mochas chatting in cafes
Sunday has a sensory unique to its array

A Gardener's Ear

Green anatomy beckons
  Abstract of another world
    Transformed in micro seconds
      To nurture my spirit swirled

    Buried deep in botany
    Seeds and roots and soil
  A time without dichotomy
A kingdom without turmoil

A tree with many arms
  And fingers that caress
    Embraced within her charms
      My treasure of tenderness

    One petal at a time
    My roses harbor my heart
  An affair with wild thyme
Can't tell humans apart

Plants are a lovers queue
  That never acts with spite
    Your feelings it construes
      Soothes your Fahrenheit

    To plants I give my love
    They whisper verse in my ear
  I am their morning dove
They are my Shakespeare

Sand Creates

Tepid fine powder regresses
Fawning feet and tickling toes
To the edge of sanity's impulses
The terrain of revision flows

Texture of a different reality
Colorful healing enzymes
Messaging the body's esprit
While mending the aging mind

To hypnotize existing shape
And summons enduring traits
Let abuses of time escape
You are what sand creates

By letting abuses of time escape, you shed your
biological age and its environmental impact.
When this happens, you engage a new existence
based on you interactions with the sands of time.

Ocean's Cradle

The privilege of drifting
Between the perpetual swells
Fluid of temporal changes
Swaying in rhythm compels

Alkaline salty air
Crisp cool breeze pristine
Endless views aqua blue
Womb like rocking machine

Floating body graces
The ocean's recasting charms
Renewed and renovated
Reborn in liquid arms

West coast is my abode
Tide pools nostalgic wand
Sea anemones, coral and urchins
Ocean's cradle yet spawned

Gazing the distance to shore
Where contrived reality cries
Umbilical cord released
Envy of those less wise

Essence of aqua pura
Time waits for us on the sea
Completing destiny's cycle
Nature's fate for thee

Eden of Edges

The desert jewel of crimson charm
Saguaros quills with open arms
Golden glitter of the searing star
Crystal air so fair for views afar

Grand Canyon's rugged daggers bloom
Descending in her jagged womb
Breathe and balance in her wedges
Eden's echo of endless edges

Sheep and snakes nap in the sun
Condors swoop and play begun
Hikers exhausted, faceless, shock
A day of stamina made of rock

Mystery's maze of primitive paths
I evolve the esteem of explorers past
Kissed by the abyss two miles deep
Embraced by earth's enigma I keep

Shaky Grounds

Lodged upon a sloping hilltop
  Overlooking slated rooftops
Dreaming of dancing
Across them all

Sun is dawning color
Visualizing ahead
Exploding sound of train
Stirring under bed

Screaming and vile it rages
Basements pipes loud roar
Bed begins to rotate
About the wavy floor

Kitchen cabinets open wide
Dishes bounce and fly
Shattered self esteem
Gravity shouts and cries

Rocket through the air
Pierce the outside pores
Undulating earth
Walking needs an oar

Tranquility on a timer
Shaky grounds warp and bend
Psycho peeling trauma
Just California my friend

Wings of My Heart

Songbirds come to my perch
And sing to me in the morning
Eyes gushing me all the while
Adoring me into their charming

Twigs of a nest is their home
Garnished in my back garden
I hovered as they were hatching
And imprinted into my stardom

Enticed by my every movement
They capture and chat when can
They nestled a corner of my heart
Just by resting on my hand

The energy of two lives in flight
Curves of a mystery meaning
A subtle and wonderful delight
Regrets to start the weaning

Its time to rally my roots
We gather to say goodbye
I grieve for love with animals
I'll look for their hearts in the sky

Golden Gate Park

Windswept dunes of sand
Carving up your face
Thousand tearful acres
Moon like lonely grace

McLaren's grand pageantry
Spawning seeds of wonder
Bleeding from his heart
Legacy's toil of thunder

Earthquake erupted fliers
Drama's bag of tricks
Breath life into the breathless
Tent city 1906

A journey of nature's gems
Rustic oasis embrace
Majestic designed museums
Heart beat dancing apace

Lagoons for sailing lost
Sculptures of artists play
Culture for nursing milk
Playground of memories stay

Terrain of lusty jade
Plotted inside my veins
Evolves my genetic code
To plant based human strains

Dancing on Clouds

I dance on clouds
In echoes of feet
In pendulum of arms
Rhythms of heartbeats

I dance on clouds
In congas of chest
In engine of legs
Melting thoughts crest

I dance on clouds
In seasons of vision
In waterfalls of brow
Endorphins in collision

I dance on clouds
Engulfed with theme
Exhausted and reborn
In screams of esteem

Just replace the word "dance" with "run" when re-reading. Screams of esteem are my take on a workout of improvement.

Windows of Wakefulness

I feel layers of time on purple pine trees
I hear melodies of birds on liquid breeze

     I see the solar fingers of a radiant haze
     I'm a wakeful window of nature's maze

I see the shadows of people who passed
I hear their vague voices as openly cast

     I feel their presence as energy remains
     I'm a wakeful window of passing domains

I see the earth as a maternal heart beating
I hear the oxygen of existence free breathing

     I feel my voltage melt morphing mankind
     I'm a wakeful window of genetic design

I can see through you

River Rafting

A summer's sear to liquid snow
Ripping rivers of daring disguise
Birds and flow capture the ears
Sun's reflection dazzles the eyes

The seduction of opium leaps
A rubber raft for a dauntless duo
Who naively navigate adrenalin
To nomad this teasing tempo

Rope tied around these torsos
Affixed to the flimsy float
With a gutsy giggling girlfriend
To the rapids we shall remote

The serenity of sailing on clouds
Gives way to excitement erupting
Swifter and swifter we swirl
Until the boom disrupting

Driven and dragged underwater
By the rapids of fabled force
Solo rope is the road to the surface
My partner is still a dark horse

As I clutch to a branch of fear
This burden buries her under
I succumb and we swim to shore
Finagling the fate of blunder

After 40 years, this close call is forever floating
inside my mind and the reason I don't take cruises.

Swooping Seagulls

A chilly chime to the day's dawning
  A boney breeze and sounds of crow
    Gliding and whirling on drifts and lifts
      Swooping seagulls are fractures of flow

      A ragtag trio of fellows
        Grey and white with golden fringe
        Angling to neb the morsels
          Forever swooping to impinge

Their harvest haunts in a buckled bag
  With leverage of the long leap bill
    They yank and drag and bust the fag
      While dancing to display their skill

      Their cheer obscures in a carton
        Enclosed, encased and entombed
          They seize a stick and pry it open
          A genius of dining plume

*I'm in awe of the artistry of these agile acrobats
and I'm impressed by their surprising ingenuity.*

Fisherman's Wharf

I yearn to watch the merchant boats
Depart from their birth to satin sea
Old mariners of weathered coats
Still pirate and pan a cult century

I yearn to be this pungent wharf
Salmon, shrimp and sand dabs
My inner child strives to morph
To a salty breeze of cauldron crabs

I yearn to banquet the chapel bench
Perched at the embarcadero's end
A little girl's soft heart to clench
And cuisine on sour dough blend

I yearn to trigger teases of yore
To preserve my daughter's clever
Be garnished by fisherman's lore
And haven this heaven forever

Venice Beach

Tie-dye surf from a rainbow hue
Reflecting through these prism eyes
Pacific sands are magnets to mind
Each grain is a hormone in disguise

A ménage of mangled origins
Swimmers, bathers and skaters
Impostors of slanted intents
Landscaping as love's invaders

For others it's a swagger in sand
Or sliders at the Sidewalk Cafe
Boutiques are a moody mall
Street acts are a daffy display

The canals are a fairy tale of time
For nomads with a nautical potions
Crews on cannabis are uncanny
Wobbling with each waxing motion

But, Venice is more than a beach
Bohemians speak reggae
An alternative freedom of style
For the hippies of modern day

Chapter Five: In Honor of Walt Whitman

*"Re-examine all that you have been told...
dismiss that which insults your soul."*

Content for the Bard

Scholars of Whitman will note that his tendency for rhyme and meter was not a characteristic of his style since this is what he rebelled against. He is sometimes called the Father of Free Verse, yet not his original child. His style was to extend and manipulate it to enhance his position as the center of the universe. This style is one of my inspirations, with the addition of some meters o mine, and is our likeness of thought.

Mirrors of Time

Snowy edges every morning and the chilly froth
throughout the day

The sounds of hammer and nails, woods and pieces,
and perspiration dripping loudly

A week of dark halos without the luster of the sun or
the brightness of thought

Each day turns into itself again as hope hypnotically
echoes the yields of yore

Facial clocks wrinkled by the passage of paces
are without expressions

I see an eerie emptiness in their eyes and hark the
tones of the ignored

It's just another social fabric that weaves our minds
into mirrors of time

O Walt Whitman

O take my hand Walt Whitman!
You are the bravest and boldest with a quill
Stood tall for poverty and poetry rejection
To champion free verse for social goodwill

Rhyming is a stepchild still roaming within
Your egocentric leanings undress us lost beings
To carve a commentary of society's fatal flaws
To take pride of healing from cathartic feelings

We know your soul is your alter ego's best friend
So, you dine with death since it's not the end
Critiques are your realism and cuisine of your shrine
Your legacy OUTSHINES what your soul has
defined

*Whitman's first publication of Leaves of Grass in 1855
was not well received since it violated traditional form.
Critics thought it was cut up prose pretending to be verse.*

Inside a Rebel's Mind

To reject the status quo
is a passage of inner discovery.

To protest slanted social standards
is the fiber of moral existence.

To view expired artistic masters
as a suspended animation of time.

To ponder scientific breakthroughs
as just one agenda of evolution.

To criticize the world's overlords
as demagogues of opportunism.

To challenge traditional education
as the fools that form the folly.

To embrace the nature of humanity
as the mindset enhancing freedom.

To question each breath you take
as oxygen that never existed before.

To be inside a rebel's mind
you must first discard your skin.

Beauty Beckons from Afar

Beauty beckons from afar in the jealousy of a pirate penthouse.
The bouquet of unconscious seeking is a chamber of the past. Inhaling wisdom of an erupting era unites my tongue and drifting ways.
The ecstasy of new ideas will always gust our breeze.

Thriving in a civil circus tempers our fraying freedoms. Bemused by the bohemian beggars with cell phones and cappuccinos in their hands.
Churning circles around the crowd is game of lost creations. Stylish societies unknowingly repeat the cycles of salty imperfections.

The dogmas in your dreams are demons of conformity.
We accept that the dependent nature of man relies on a cosigned character.
And we crave the impulse of energy that seeks the integrity of insight.
Life is an envy of beauty that beckons from afar,

Always out of reach.

Live Once More

We live once more
To enlighten ourselves
To revive and re-conceive
To learn human lessons
To become deeper and apt
To belong and evolve

We have been designed
Unaware of the blueprint
Hiding in your genes
Spoken by your soul
Arranged by archetype
Liquefies your nature

We are social fragments
Passing through the past
Envious for a future
Bonding lurid loneliness
Morphing to conform
Borrowing an identity

We fold over upon ourselves
Living epitome of ancestry
Talking to us from behind
The same appalling message
We dangle from these strings
Until we live once more

Now That I'm Aged

Now that I'm aged, I must dream
Like acrobats losing vintage angles
My body slowly dissolves its mission
Departure's doors are dormant for now
I grind a game of deception with myself
Vagary visions that don't exist on earth
Just to silence the ignorance
                    of the unknown

The length of your mind alters your attitude
Only time is designed to recover prior pieces
Embryo days meander by with enabled ease
I strive to move the motions of priorities
To marbleize meaning out of thin air
While construing time into
                    life spans of rhymes

A blank social slate keeps the heart in hiding
So I regress to a tinsel time of belonging
When insignificance was of utmost importance
And what is important is not yet perceived
Each day is another wisp of this wisdom
Now that I'm aged,
                    I must dream

When Bald Eagles Cry

To Protest is to stand in the rain
And stare down broken mirrors
Reflecting the tainted targets
Of corrupted histories of time

To Protest is an internal journey
To the hallow of a heavy heart
And a mind that's crystallized
To shoot arrows of rebellion

To Protest is a new morality
That boils the black blood
Of fearful regressed minds
Into fagots of the forgotten

To Protest is an awakening
A sage for advancing society
Hedging humanity into balance
Through integrity of your genes

*This is in support for all the children protesting gun
violence. Hope is on your side and so are millions.*

Unmask Your Mind

To pardon my captive cohorts forever grasping
behind me
   for a shrinking sense of self.

Squirming for dire directions is a tantrum of the inner
child
   seeking an secure identity.

Fragments of broken faces and painfully hidden ages
   are regressing to digest.

We enable our core of esteem to amend this
   tempest of fearful thoughts.

My character of fair climates coos in its vaulted
cavern
   waiting to echo and evolve.

My compass is a hope for future wisdom as
   measured by the insight of culture.

Arising from social cocaine is this vigor of freedom
   that unmasks your mind.

Bard of Democracy

Alone and adrift on a snowy park bench
White hair throwing verse to the breeze
Captured by the rapids of his scribing
Unaware of the monkey at his knees

Pensive people creatively unparalleled
Cultivates my tendency to trespass
I shape into him unnoticed and unknown
And recite his lyrics of requiem mass

He's the voice of the doomed and departed
From servants of poverty and hypocrisy
With a maestro mind and haunted heart
He thrives as the bard of democracy

Whitman was described as the first American "bard of democracy." He extended his value system into his work against slavery and for women's and immigrant rights.

Optical Illusions

Your primrose path for liberty is hidden
    in dark caverns of the disguised

Blind is admiration of image collectors
    who characterize a theatrical affair

Family fluency is a horse and carriage of
    genetic history on concrete beds

To hover with Wall Street's caged souls
    is money weeping the loudest social lie

The towers of ideology that redesign the sky
    trick the inner self into an outer dogmas

Denying society's scope of optical illusion
    is freedom's view of truth

Six: Transformational Locations

We all have favorite places in our hearts that bring up specific meaning and emotion. The location we call home becomes symbolic of how we feel and a reflection of our identity. Each location has a unique quirkiness that creates its own mental landscape.

To travel is to stimulate ancestral rituals that evolve subconscious character.

Baghdad by the Bay

Enchantment of the bay
Echoing ships wax and wane
Cuisine for kings quell any fray

Hills and valleys to wander lost
Cable cars that kiss the stars
Wind and cold till Spartans exhaust

From the wild and gay stormy free
To the liberal and rebellious profound
We are the climate of style degrees

From rekindling roots of tread
To connecting the dangling traits
I am the City inborn and inbred

Mosaics of lost people and places
Floating in the air like balloons
Generations of memory laces

To refresh internal enzymes
Restoring my muse to revolve
Your home is your identity in time

Compass Cafes

The pungent aroma of roasted beans
The chit chatter of human art
Gurgling of the espresso machine
Liquid warmth for my
lonely heart

Cafes carve a parallel zone
Characters contrived from another time
European rituals for the lingering unknown
Poet in the corner lost
in rhyme

Open invitation to a sacred sphere
Compass cafes are savvy to condone
Social lures are captions to cohere
Society's bohemian
backbone

I'm charmed by my cappuccino
Who whispers sweet verse in my ear
That transforms me into Thoreau
To debate with my buddy
Shakespeare

Streets of Texture

Sunday rounds of Berkeley
Roaming streets of textures
Inside this cycle of culture
Ivory towers of roman stone
Constantly changing faces
Student bodies of microchips
Designing inside their heads
Like genies hiding in a urn
Dreaming of a timely return

People's Park of animation
The beat of an Indian tabla
And clang of manjerra cymbals
Dancers colored into fabrics
Woven under the sunshine
Spicy aroma tingles your body
Pineapple curry, Thai cuisine
A passage to a foreign land
And ecstasy of orphan glands

Homelessness is given a bone
Forming identities in a hollow
To the library of discarded prints
Taking free books, not baths
Byron, Cummings, and Shelley
Verse is the violated vogue
To abandon the art of bards
I accept these books as treasures
That weave me streets of textures

Le Train de Vin

To hear the clatter of iron wheels
And swoon the sway of soft surreal
To seek this virtue of Victorian vogue
And mint my heart as revolving rogue
To glamour the aroma of galley's design
And feel the softness of vintage wines
To tour the nature of Napa's nurture
While evolving to epicure searcher
To taste the tenderness of the train
And celebrate our bond to
champagne
To harbor
the hand
of equal rhyme
While toasting a triumph of lifetime

*A romantic sojourn to Napa Valley with a special heart
provides an emotional memory for a lifetime. The wine
train was gourmet cuisine paired with the right vintage in
a time capsule of the 1880s Victorian era. If you're ever in
the area, it's your memory too.*

Expressionism

An artful deviation of colorful resistance
An international meeting of friends to existence

Foreign and familiar drink the cocktail to ascend
Maestro minds beckon to fantasy and amend

Fusing infant innocence to elders edging away
San Francisco's under belly is a festive display

Radical reflections in mirrors of gay pride
From birthday suits to rainbows in my eyes

Closet doors of doubters are suddenly unhinged
Liberty's open fringe is the melting pot linchpin

Raw self-expression is explosive wit inbred
Social acceptance is now a partner in your bed

In 2017, I attended the San Francisco Gay Pride 47th Festival of Folly. An opportunity to dress up and act silly to advance a social agenda is always photo and verse worthy.

College

To minds and memories, rules and truth
Higher standards, ageless youth

To years and beers, caps and gowns
Strength of coffee, sleepless frowns

To grades and shades, dorms and havens
Teenage tempers, motley mavens

To bytes and windows, cookies and worms
Digital daze, scheduling squirms

To teachers and terms, clubs and class
Being broke, smoking grass

To plans and futures, English and math
Social sophomores, primrose path

School of Verse

A school of toddlers thrives next to me
    Society's playground of dreams carefree

Each day the window opens my heart
    Innocence laughs and screams Descartes

Young moving montage of make believe
    Is the dawn of ideas up my sleeve

Original fantasy is the mind's vanguard
    And the bard's academy of avant-garde

I become an elf to infuse myself
    While my trite identity lurks on the shelf

I grind my mind and bride my verse
    To regress a character to traverse

The Traveler

I'm a marksman for mystery
In the marrow of my bones
Dauntless for strange domains
Obliging the obscure and unknown

It's not a veranda of vitality
Nor a feather for social wings
It's the rhapsody of your realism
And the occult for offspring

Eclipsing the edge of the eagle
Chopsticks, kimonos and matcha
These skies have turned to crimson
Caressed by culture of Buddha

Back tracking to early history
When gentry was sculpted from stone
Where Aristotle once angled
And gave science a backbone

Antiquities and ancient times
Lessons from the origin of thought
Particles of ironic perceptions
To question all that we're taught

My Dad's Café

My sister and I
At father's favorite flavor
Dining for nostalgia of time
Fragments of feelings to savor

Enveloped by memory's feast
Curiosity erupting to expand
Catching lost hearts to connect
Like a seabird in search of land

The warmth of a particle presence
An eeriness swarming my space
From the vast vault of heaven
To his energy messaging my face

This is a rite of passage
To tempt the temperature of time
To learn and clever this custom
While escorting eternity's rhyme

Dad's cafe is Tad's Steakhouse on Powell Street
that the family has frequented since the 1960s.

My Daughter's Room

In my daughter's room
Is a sanctuary for my senses
A heavenly serenity surrounds me
And evaporates all my defenses

Camping in college till summer
Memories are painting these walls
Photos and drawings and poetry
On the bed is her first baby doll

Temptations of a time portal
History is ushered with urgency
From missing her so intensely
To harvesting vintage circuitry

I read and become her renderings
The passions of a unique heirloom
Reshapes me into her character
In my daughter's room

Seattle   Return

Fairy
tales explode the
scale, When your
slate is envy eight. Silent trains
on a single rail, Floating above estates.
Elevator to the sky, A heaven love creates.
Cuisine to deify, Reserved for those ornate.
Carnival rides to climb, Screaming
on fairgrounds. I had a
pretending time, In my
hope for clowns.
Asleep in
memory's
womb,
Child
hood
dreams
amask
Time to
r a t t le
the tomb,
Fifty years
have passed.
Avail the inner
child, Fish market
and terrain. Intricate
memories smiled, Even
their face and names. Vistas
of soaring birdlife, Hover the sky
monorail. Completing circles of life

My existential cocktail.

*For my bucket list, I returned to Seattle after 50 years to
finally ride the Monorail and dine in the Space Needle.*

Haight Ashbury

Victorians of a virtuous era
Style of a gilded drift
Climate of liberal thought
Weather of paradigm shift

Hippies are the sidewalks
Expanding side by side
Tattered tie-dye patterns
Children once decried

Darkness circles their eyes
Confusion drips their face
Trembling hands splash
For any gifted grace

Home is a relic prison
Symbolically left behind
Trampled in oppression
Freedom is fugitive to find

It's a velocity of evolution
Bound by the value of virtue
New ideals stem solutions
Covet for a keener future

Thinkers molding society
Crypt to tyrannical fate
At this pivotal birthplace
The summer of '68

*Summer of 1968 was my first trip to the Haight Ashbury
that opened my mind and forged an indelible impression.*

Hotel of Fragments

Castles and regal estates
Thriving in suburban marrow
Heartland of high stakes

Hunger drowns in the pond
Catering from dawn till dusk
Duty of turning vagabonds

Staffed with eagles eyes
To read the slightest faux pas
Quick to realign any flaws

Lightness of day is pall
Room and board is shared and small
Acquiescence is the golden rule for all

Hotel of fragmented dreams
Losing yourself demands valor
Of alter ego extremes

Acquired sojourn that bleeds
Caught in a cage of prey
Scream loudly for prior misdeeds

Peering through grey bars of strife
Breathing with breathless life
Thought is the only remnant still bright

Mardi Gras

Your hidden ego's vogue on theatrical tour
For masquerade's exotic and hypnotic lure

Identity of amnesia is timely interlaced
Whimsy of incognito is yours to embrace

Sling the heavy grind way and far behind
Social gravity now stylishly unconfined

An orgy of crowd, drink and Cajun cuisine
Spirits of Casanova are dripping obscene

Jubilees of jazz seducing a body sweet
Open intoxication tumbles down the street

French Quarter's balconies of iron charm
Help hedonist with bare breasts disarm

Stroke of midnight is the key to conform
Crowds vaporize to passing windstorms

*This is one of the few times and places where an "off
center universe" is the norm. When Mardi Gras is over at
the stroke of midnight, everyone suddenly drops their
drinks and returns home like robots, like they vaporized.*

Chinatown

Tasseled lanterns sway
Oval for harmony's delight
Heartfelt humble of ages
Red symbols of pride ignite

Windows of Beijing ducks
With roasted necks so long
Nestled with chicken and geese
Cuisine of Asian throngs

Imperial slanted roofs
Figures of crouching beasts
Planted quite symbolically
Dutiful rituals of east

To the love of art's bazaar
Gold Buddhas, silk and jade
The orient's exotic mingle
Shades within the parade

Hunan and Sichuan styles
Spiced in another sphere
Startles body and mind
Chop sticks laughing tears

Ancestry of saving face
Framed on respect and pride
Confucius glues the culture
The envy of those less wise

Berkeley Campus

The sky is crystal clear and rays of thought are sheer
The motion of jagged joggers ventures nimble near

Fluid of sweaty bodies glistens in a radiant rain
Redwoods of light and shade dazzle the optic plane

A mingling of castle minds shaded by octopus oak
Captured by an elder with heavy words he spoke

The roar of roasted coffee is aroma of the mind
The percolating of ideas to incline mankind

A group of tactful talents is quakes in the quad
Painting signs to cure and counter social fraud

"Say it loud and clear, foreigners are welcome here"
Our high road to cohere and humanity to endear

There is a special atmosphere of freedom and optimism
coalescing on certain campuses. U. C. Berkeley tends
be the epitome of progressive thought, self-expression,
and personal growth.

Library of Lives

Preceding the digital daze
A romance of parchment with ink
That authored my second home
And cataloged my thoughts in sync

With a personality so palatial
A respite rich from poverty
Consoled from the claws of cold
From hopelessness to scholarly

It's the sanctuary for my mind
A Sheppard for youth's curiosity
An absolute for my aptitude
And a road for social velocity

As a child I sailed Kon-Tiki
Into Charlotte's Web I ran
I hovered with Huckleberry Finn
And even ate Green Eggs and Ham

The heart of harmony lay open
To the sounds of vintage imagery
I first meandered with Mozart
Then Stravinsky's symphony

Now this abstract is archived
Courtship is to copy this love
Praise for this shelter to thrive
My savior sage from above

Musée du Louvre

Intensity is burning brown eyes
　Poetically piercing my heart
A sheer and fragile veil of elves
Waves of her auburn mane part

Her fame is Mona Lisa
As she whispers into your wander
She shelters you into her sacred
To massage you into a ponder

The entombed Egyptian rooms
Sequels from the Stone Age
Pharaohs of superhuman size
Seized by Napoleon's rampage

We toga to the Roman Empire
And touch the Caesars of the time
Bronze and marble and terra-cottas
Vibrations that vortex your spine

The radiance of Rembrandt rages
His realism is larger than life
He melts you into his quagmire
And seduces your into his wife

Medieval fortress to paragon palace
Surviving the taboos of time
An ideal window of parallel travel
And a slice of heaven to rhyme

Kalifornia

This land where mountains marble to heaven
    And endless shorelines bank and beckon
Where the garden soil is subject to sermon
    Crops are worshiped like boundless bourbon

This land of talented egos and topples
    Where the daring can caper colossal
Invoked innovation brings eerie esteems
    Rags to riches seek rugged routines

This land to barter for sultry beach beauties
    With fascinations for talent and movies
Who abandon past people and parcels
    Are trick takers for morsels of marvels

This land is a wonder for cycles of change
    Where novel attitudes abridge the estranged
Silicon Valley is the future of fate
    Oafish outsiders steam heartburn and hate

This land where I derive, roam and rant
    Despite traffic, taxes and transplants
With foresight, beauty and brilliance
    Your mind awakens to eco-resilience

Lost Angeles

Our Lady the Queen of Angels
Fraction departed years ago
Rescinding all Godly spells

Tarnished by social implosion
Sardines of piranha crowds
Reshapes ambition's motion

Your passage is locust swarms
Hindering any sense of compass
A challenge of temper's storms

Smog and sulfate life robust
Breathe and choke and seethe
A brown metal blanket of dust

Vice and gangs playground
Beware the senseless tomb
Compromised life if found

Yet, armies of seekers still arrive
The fiscally desperate and fallen
Seek teeth and claws to survive

Struggle and bleed to the end
Second and third chance society
Designed for faults of frantic trends

Chapter Seven: Existential Experiences

Existential experiences are interaction between novel situations and unexpected emotions that push the envelope of human understanding. To experience this anguish or ecstasy from the inside out, let go of all your preconceived notions and allow yourself to flow like liquid down life's waterfall.

To rapture the next meaning is to startle your hidden passions into dancing with your dreams.

Frames of Reference

The Belly of Being

Let your dreams
infuse you
quake you
remake you

Change your world
in design
in purpose
in entirety

Reverse your history
of mistakes
of thought
of existing

Become larger than life
to wisdom
to compete
to survive

Carve your personality
in motions
in minds
in stone

Preserve your destiny
of identity
of being
of rebirth

Question for You

Do you feel subtly disconnected
Not yourself or somebody rare?

Do you want to escape this reality
Of dos and don'ts and affairs?

Do you wish to be wonderfully wealthy
Not toiling or taking or game?

Do you hunger for a genius mind
Rather than slave to dogmas of fame?

Do you view society as scheming
Not fair or equal or of trust?

Do you crave unconditional love
Rather than revolving door lust?

Do you long to live in human time
Not the clock or sun or moon?

Do you dream to evolve in a sphere
Rather than hide in a pleasant cocoon?

Silence of a Missing Part

Loud silence of an elusive embrace
I'll pillage for a gallant gear
To epoch this lonely space
And master this phantom fear

Each day I'm a briefcase
I pretend I'm so refined
Hidden deep is a liquid face
Gasping in cryptic confines

My mind is not a hungry heart
Nor a frenzy for friends
Loud silence of a missing part
An identity I can't transcend

Orbits of obscured answers
Malingering in our minds
Emptiness leaves a mild cancer
And a gap for all mankind

The search for reality

Birthdays

To the rites of cultural passions
Most coveted of celebrations
The only holiday you own
And the rebirth of incarnations

A private passage of insight
From one year to the next
An accumulation of attitudes
For the debt of time to perplex

The paradox of lost perspectives
Mentality is the monster within
In youth, it's yardsticks and yodels
With age, it gets under your skin

To the harvest of all prior wisdom
And to valor the fates of maturity
Mint your mind to the eventual
Not sentiments of past security

Each birthday is a dawn of destiny
For that we shout and serene
Past lessons are hands of heaven
And carpe diem is self-esteem

*Many of us turn birthdays into an existential crisis of
needed confirmation from others that lead to anxious
vulnerability. I prefer to embrace birthdays as new
beginnings.*

Whispers on the Wind

The glow of early horizon
Orange and purple and blues
Meandering through the meadow
Petite white daisies of shoes

Feet drinking the morning dew
A white shadow acrobat
Displaying his deviations
Summons me to chat

An uncanny vortex of venue
Triggered by this place in time
Who passed away a year ago
Who whispers wrinkled rhymes

We hover and habit awhile
Who calls me from time of place
To pull me out of my shell
And eclipse me with embrace

*When you reach a certain age, you bid farewell to people
and their memories, but accept them when they return.*

Maestro of Meaning

Time's mystery of fugitive meaning
I'm swamped with quagmire questions
To the true tenure of my existence
And the purpose of self-expressions

Fables fly the answer in religion
But faith is not the factual life
Science seeks to measure reality
Yet fails to explain senseless strife

Life spans are so fragile and fleeting
With time so misplaced and elusive
Whatever energy drives your essence
Demands diligence to stay exclusive

If you submit your soul to sail the ship
Each utility will unfold unscripted
If your mind and body connect to time
To the maestro of meaning you drifted

Personality Particles

Self defined by high exposures
So anguish can compass my way
I induce my intent to swell so vast
So imagination can shrink your day

I expose your shame and sins
And heartless traits of appeal
I undress your security of being
While sculpting your life surreal

I'll particle your personality
And steal ancestral insights
I'll unhinge your sense of integrity
Just to thrill my reader's delights

The Fringe

I'm on the edge of reality
With kaleidoscope eyes
Fracturing pending people
Dissecting their disguise

Mind of a colorful mosaic
Heart of a costumed child
The ego of a risk taker
Society's rules exiled

My off center universe
Propelling me to extremes
Closing the curtains on tradition
My fringe of creative dreams

Capitalist Caper

Social
savvy for the agile
Rave philosophy for the rich
A fairy tale for the fortunate
Lopsided is the
glitch

Competition
shapes the caper
A defeat and defend society
Where intel and ability are vital
And failure marries
anxiety

Survives
not a superior system
To motivate humans to excel
Where conflict defines survival
To flourish under this
spell

Mirage

A toddler tempered gypsy
ascending her comfort zone
chasing a
      moving
           ménage.

Indulged with juggling debris
from imagined romantic fallouts
while grasping for
          future's
             corsage.

A future of bumpy bones
without the map of the heart
are seductive
      pieces of
          montage.

The call of children faded
silencing dark clouds of time
are shadows
      of the next
          mirage.

Verse in a Bottle

Floating in thoughts of years
Nurturing lost tempers of mine
Seeking to buoy my message
To carve an alternative time

An ageless rock of personal pride
Inspired by extremes of existence
My opinions to orbit continually
So scribing can evoke resistance

Verses of woven wisdom
In a capsule of space and time
All dreams, feelings and being
In a chronicled rendition of rhyme

It's my note in the bottle of life
Noteworthy of valiant is verse
Evolving myself into the globe
I am the course of the universe

The Mood of Money

If the mood of money is vaulted esteem
And sense of self is morality resigned
If net worth is an edge of euphoria
Narcissism has marauded your mind

If finagling funds is a duty of pride
And mogul meaning is coveted art
If cagey schemes are lures of loves
Sociopathy has hybrid your heart

If common people are stepping stones
And dollars determine your cagey cohort
If you yearn for a mentality of money
You've sold your soul to yet extort

Cocoons of the Tuned

Little people standing tall in an acid rain
Dogma's ugly tongue is their acid of pain
Mindless leaders take domains to repossess
Thoughtless plunders of arrows to regress

Character flaws flourish in social reality
Patterns of the clever hiding in the sea
Creative cultures twisting to the ultra tuned
Eclipse of evolution concealing in cocoons

*I'm in a society that places capitalism above knowledge
and human progress to keep the status quo. This results in
hidden pockets of scientists and free thinkers increasingly
banning together in private endeavors.*

Reinvent Yourself

To awaken my hidden self
Each morning I ravage the rust
When imagination is your zen
Each future is breaking the crust

Climbing out of my skin
To hover above this maze
Ports of purpose have no address
Times of intent have no praise

When creativity is your campaign
Your chorus cannot encore
The course of your character
Fractures for fate to explore

From harvesting a maniac mind
To the insanity to transcend
The banality of binary beings
To reinvent myself again

Why Are We Here?

To question existence itself
The enigma of why we are
Masquerade like answers
To wisdom's elusive star

Society labels and curbs you
Relative to fear of traits
And roaming culture queues
Defines how shear your fate

Identity locks your prison
Umbrella around your mind
Mandates a molded mask
Your genesis is confined

Personality is a video
From inside out and back
It's your virtuoso of deviations
And your climate's cognac

Why is a lingering question
Temporal patterns of change
Just sunlight and reflection
Your photons to arrange

Existence loves mutation
The evolution of your mind
From genetics to behavior
No meaning left behind

L. S. D.imensions

Animated mentality, the damsel of designs
Sharp experiments off cliffs of hungry minds

Your alter ego sings, hidden thoughts expand
It's liquid freedom you're sipping from your hand

Artifacts of childhood, other worldly poise
Memory cells recast to superficial noise

In thought misdirection, you forgo its control
It mangles perceptions and wanders your soul

Fractured word fringes, a delusional exchange
Bemused into existing outside reality's range

A parade of cosmic shapes, melting your head
Kaleidoscopic vision is the partner in your bed

To the fantasy of seekers, it's not godhead
It's simply psychedelic as your insight is misled

*I experimented with LSD when in college and found it
to be an exercise in anxiety management. Perceptions
are so intensely distorted for so long that you crave
and appreciate just getting back to normal.*

Reluctant Eyes

Merging to the mender
Cloaked behind the window
Stolen but a child
Reluctant eyes in limbo

Fractured by the facade
White and cold and hard
Lingering deep in my heart
Grim reaper's calling card

Twisted by the tempo
Head throbbing in reverse
Time to disrobe your soul
Barks the deadpan nurse

The oxygen of obituaries
Inhaling tubes of meaning
I'll scream dreamlessly
Heedless of the gleaning

Darkness is my anthem
Filleted on a metal bed
Vexing what might crumble
 If my maker and I break bread

The dawn escorts my eyes
Echoes tickle my ears
From hovering above the abyss
To a phoenix of new frontiers

Running Without Feet

To the images of easy gliding
On the courage of gusty winds
And dreams of avid soaring
On my feet of little wings

To inherit a stallion's gallop
And harness tenacious pride
To redeeming tools of traits
For maturing steps of stride

When the world goes awry
I compass the clever cleats
Wisdom is adhesive to time
As freedom is fleetness to feet

Gift of virtue above the clouds
Yet, celebration is overcast
The dawn of my winter's body
Now storming with contrasts

Old bones like peanut brittle
Spent legs are bulky bookends
I'm reduced to fossil fantasy
To parody the years to pretend

Sprawling meadows and forests
Phantoms of a past heartbeat
To the spirit of vicarious running
Without the kiss of my feet

Doors of Perception

I thirst for the fluid of gray liquid matter
I crave to pass through humanity's walls
Unhinging the doors of subliminal perception
To experience reality of reversed protocols

I feel the passing particles of light and air
And the novel insights eclipsing past impair
Odd opportunities are now open synergies
The micro doors of energy are perception aware

Unraveling the beauty of the universe is vision
Through doors, people, and atoms of all kinds
Peaceful innovation is portal of our purpose
The doors of perception evolve in our minds

Hippie Vision

Born into a society opposing evolution
Dire fear of strange is clothing their confusion

Peace and acceptance, our elastic gloves
Truth and equality, our fallen loves

Surfing minds of change feeds the fiery fuel
Protests and rebellion, the remedy of tools

Shed the pirate's plan of world leaders brutality
Integrity is a flower child's gift and morality

Birth of global unity dwarfs dictator confines
Political sheep dangle behind harbinger minds

We seek a new dimension to expand novel thought
To open mental wormholes as the future is sought

*I believe the old hippy vision of peace and love, equality
and acceptance, of all divergent people is marbled within
a modern society still struggling to find its identity.*

Window People

Long tooth man guiding cart
Robbed of speech and gauge
Blind to other socials
Adrift within his cage, betrayed

Sagging child floats behind
Ghost mother sails ahead
 Mesmerized by her phone
Toddler's lonesome dread, dejected

Fidgety matron clutches dearly
Her dog of talk and play
Dresses extra frumpy
Life screams of yesterday, fixated

 Limping Chinese lady
 Hollow eyes, droopy face
Perched alone each day
Language barrier waste, isolated

Gaunt and trembling fellow
Bleeds to stop and chat
Chilling desperate diary
Affect always flat, anxious

For all the perishing people
Their crimes I'll never steal
 Death of life's amazements
To trite routine ordeals, surreal

Saving Face

My saving face is scholarly
My philosophy to explore
Screams and fear from poverty
And squirming on the floor

The quake of determination
Angst of ancestral collapse
From an expiration of knowledge
Into time without elapse

From birthing to authorship
Time's urgency is finite
To seize opportunity's grip
And alter psychology's rites

A duty of character strength
To express your genetic code
Freedom drives its length
Hunger conquers its road

The air of our existence
Is a breeze of identity
The personality of persistence
Is an epic of legacy

Stock Market

From tears of toiling for a whittled wage
To minds of hoping for a savior sage

Allure of easy riches fathers fantasy
Of grand estates and vaulted vanity

The ecstasy of winning elates you to extol
The agony of losing deflates a sagging soul

These random movements, so counter intuitive
Even magic mortals can't prevent the punitive

Vendors vying to be your money's mentor
Their success is your maniac misadventure

Rogue responsible for your dire disaster
Silent laughter defines the folly forecaster

So you break solo with your tacit tools
With high frequency trades and dark pools

Their racket is too rooted to share the stage
Even Satan screams and stumbles in a rage

I was a Series 7 stockbroker for five years. People don't realize how difficult and risky the market is until they languish a terrible loss that can destroy peoples' lives.

Writer's Block

Summer morning patio
Caressed by a hundred trees
Thinking with my senses
And Aristotle's breeze

Observing fluid thoughts
In a vortex around my head
My hand turns into a pencil
And scribes a verse from dead

Themes from marble masters
Reassembled by the wind
Interpreted as my mentors
Their translucence to transcend

Intuition breeds my heed
Dialogues are a séance affair
Secrets from world of wisdom
Converts me into Voltaire

Lyrical ideas of shapeless form
Returning to time and space
To evolve your writer's block
Regress to history's embrace

Homeless Hearts

Hearts of homeless shadows abound
Perishing in doorways without a sound

Forever teasing through tainted trash
Beggars to victims of social whiplash

I willfully ignored them all the time
Now I examine each facial line

I delve deeply into their ebony eyes
Curious why wonder wouldn't rise

If hate or hostility is not their host
If embarrassed enough to act a ghost

I ask if I can make their day
To fancy funds to pale their gray

A smile, a thanks, or maybe a caress
For my homeless heart to coalesce

*As a child, I was afraid of homeless people and ignored
them most of my adulthood. Now I can feel the agony
in their faces and the pain from the slump in their backs.
Deep in my heart, I feel guilty, so I try to give back.*

American Football

Pop culture's pastime of the era
Ascendency of masculine sport
An identity for your locale
That impulse of idols escort

Grand riches are incentive
Notoriety will twist and shout
Your flock will flutter forever
If you thrash and trounce about

To the virtue of pain and suffering
Of gladiators from thankless times
You're recaptured back to Rome
And coliseums of brutal rhymes

Genes of an ancestral instinct
From homo-erectus refined
Shepherd and sanctioned to swell
To keep aggression enshrined

Few values ascend so valiant
Violence is the American way
Competition ripples in the gut
In light of judgment day

I relish watching football since I was a kid. I love the speed and physicality, but every game is rife with pain and injury.

My Writing Hand

I dissect my writing hand
   Who pranks my curious construe
      With an autonomous attitude
         And desire to self-askew

Virtuous veins draw her map
   Like the amazons of my mind
      Jargon journeys for tiny travelers
         Like the blind searching to find

Each finger umpires unique
   Characters without a backbone
      And schemes of scaling critiques
         Sarcasm is how they're prone

Their drama is to delude
   Of who they insist I become
      We negotiate my latitude
         Despite obscured outcomes

My hand is my alter ego
   The subconscious part of me
      With expectations beyond myself
         Into hysteria I can't foresee

Poets of Knots

Enter not the poets of knots
For they are doors without a hinge
And knobs that do not turn
With squeaks that make me cringe

They convey a code of camouflage
Intended to obscure and mystify
Intoxicated with their own prose
While meaning has gone awry

As language labors to animate
And create a new niche of art
Extracting minds often vacate
The sweet simplicity of the heart

We all wrinkle to be novel and wise
To museum a message for all time
If passion emotes your chamber
Let creativity emote your chimes

If your form mangles your message
And decipher is a tedious task
Your true voice has been silenced
And you're hiding behind a mask

The Free Press

A prospering press scales social power
Built and protected by freedom's tower
A staged performance of mock morality
For a moving pretense of borrowed reality

Hyped headlines of seductive remarks
One liners hoax to swoon your spark
Designed to sell you a sultry sensation
And weave fake fabrics into the nation

A once higher duty to defeat hypocrisy
Yet all outlets clone the same odyssey
Pawned as pastry for hungry palates
Cooking your cake is baking your ballots

This statue of free press is cloaked today
When cagey charlatans twist their sway
The political power of corrupted force
Controls free press as puppets remorse

*I live in a time when the press is manipulated by false
news stories and political pressure to slant others. Those
in power realize the way to control the masses is via the
media which ends up undermining democracy.
I hope this is a passing phase.*

Law Enforcement

Historical crisis of confidence
Is hidden in its existence
The cornerstone of brutality
Thrives in systemic resistance

The art of deceptive facades
Campaigns to devise corruption
Reveling in the venom of racism
Watch out for gender abductions

When integrity is an idle veneer
And false reporting a fancy
Collusion is easy and cozy
While courts are just as chancy

From explicitly ending lives
To oblivious of cause or care
Manslaughter is always protected
When law enforcement is there

Welcome to society's grand impair

This is out of humble honesty after working with law enforcement in two city jails and four state prisons. Certain parts of culture are broken in ways the average person is not privy to, but later shocked by.

Wheels of War

Losing a soul mate to the wealthy's war
Rips your heart out to flounder on the floor

And empties your mind to all human kind
Until your screech and scream yourself blind

Politics or religion map its ugly cause
Barbaric genes violate nature's laws

An ideology shepherd of selfishness
Fear and paranoia seed the evilness

Patriotism is the delusion of his dying day
A sacred sanction for innocence of prey

The incompetence of man to compromise
Guarantees an existence of cries and demise

If my conclusion seems extreme, consider the historical absence of peace on the planet at any one point.

Million Kid March

Turning points defining our times
Massive school shootings of children
With worshiped weapons of war
Gun makers are minting a million

A bleeding protest of teenagers
A rejecting of political cowards
Who coddle every crazy and criminal
To buy weapons like wild flowers

Fatality's facts that scald and scar
It's a red neck and gun society
This era of life is languishing lost
Welcome to the age of anxiety

From the fisted fear of simple safety
Children are the linchpins of liberty
Of a morally bankrupted president
Who is proud to mitigate this misery

It's a bizarre social commentary
When children initiate integrity
When survival is defined by risk
And risk is defined by disparity

*My heart goes out to all those children who were lost and
to those kids marching with hearts in their hands. The USA
has the most gun violence of any country on earth.*

Idiosyncrasy

Purple sky, rainbow fields
  My vision of prisms to foresee

Warm loneliness, puppet friends
  Tinsel wilderness partakes the social tree

Hermit hearts, concrete faces
  An alienation between desire and free

Prior mistakes, altered regrets
  Leftover insights of the nth degree

Jungle legs, bouncing backbones
  Genetic resumes keep melting the brie

Inner child, elderly sage
  Surfing toward wisdom's marquee

Uncommon paces, eccentric graces
  Character champions of idiosyncrasy

Chapter Eight: Childhood Drama

This is the gut-wrenching chapter since it deals with the uneven experience of childhood. Although, difficult to write at times, the emotionally charged content is a volatile foundation of expressive poetry. To get in touch with the emotions of your inner child, write with your left hand. This activates the creative and intuitive right hemisphere of your brain.

Childhood is timeless when reality is a game while games are timeless to reality.

Inner Child Content

Rogue Van Gogh

I used to dream of being a flute
A key instrument in the band
I echo reflect their sound and suit
Until melody turned to commands

Vogue ideas are rogue Van Gogh
Creative flurries yet to define
The wit and zeal that I bestow
Abstracts the art of new design

When the menace of novel notions
Melts the marrow in their bones
They think and thrive in slow motions
While bouncing on rubber backbones

Now I'm a rebel in rainbow skin
In the garden of fear and flout
I learned it's a folly to fight to fit in
When legend is meant to stand out

Sleeping in Suitcases

I'm a
child of only six
as I look down at my plate
there is a slice of bread
and butter that
await

This is
dinner for tonight
we have no yard to grow
I feel hallow all the time
a burden of purpose
I know

Bags of
rice and beans
donated at our door
we're cursed as very different
when your fame is to
ignore

As just
a little person
I accept my social place
money makes you large
so I sleep in my
suitcase

Cycle of Character

Intoxication of youth
Style of frolic and banter
Love, autonomy, truth

Child's ascendancy dreams
Wheels explode mobility
Self empowered esteems

Master of your shape
Cheetah with borrowed legs
Identity wearing a cape

To a rebel's ego integrity
From society's mindless mimics
A cuisine that eats disparity

Hover the crowded fray
Unhinged cycle of being
Adrift my insidious way

Dismiss the people of sheep
Pedal the cycle of character
Savor the zealot they weep

Slippery Child

I am a slippery child
Roaming the streets carefree
Delight of a city squirrel
Curiosity I can't foresee

Exploring valleys and hills
Invading the city's den
Randomness of thrills
The art of childhood zen

Palace of cinema hearts
Intensions craving to bend
Money lost its smarts
I learned to sneak within

Working ladies promote
Fashions of evening ignite
Mode of staying afloat
Societies without birthrights

People of squalor life
Motley mosaic style
Wandering with this wildlife
Like riding a crocodile

Pilfer a little bourbon
Swindling with a smile
A deceptive destiny urban
I am a slippery child

Sport's Lesson

Sport is lesson's dare
Running is a style
A fashion you can wear
Designing your profile

The fracture of high school
Track team of many rhymes
Springboard's power tool
Mile relay paradigm

State finals moving fast
Our lead is now huge
Baton placed in my hand
Third leg of burning shoes

I gave the final runner
A lead he couldn't lose
Gold metal of the summer
Victory's smiling cruise

Without the slightest breeze
The sprinter falls on face
Leftovers pass with ease
The dream is now disgrace

The fleetest were last today
Relying on others beware
Team unity betrayed
Sport is lesson's dare

7th Year

To playing in the city, A child of only seven, Sound of
a friendly horn, Dash of excitement, Across rush hour
Head met with metal, Day turned to black, Spalled on the
road, Up and staggered I've been told. Light of day
returned a blur, Fireman
leaning over me, Towel
to my bloody head, All
turned to night again.
Awoke in a hospital bed,
Mother keep walking
away, My two little
sisters in tow, Claimed
too busy with them, To
worry about my woes.
Like debris brushed
aside, Never under-
stood to this day,
Easy to bring the
girls, See if my boat
drifted away. 55 years
ago that bloody day
I still feel the bump
on my head, And the
ripping of mother's empti-
ness, Like it was yesterday

Wake the Dreams

Poverty questions the future
Without status or embrace
Your origins are pre-defined
Born hollow and displaced

Life is dangling fragments
Infant eyes scarcely see
Small domain of parents
Genetic serpents of me

Breathe and seethe hunger
Innocent minds plea
Crumbs of pain for dinner
Famine's knife to flee

Broken shoe identities
Smell of forsaken screams
Clothes of antiquity
Cloak of corroded dreams

Old zombies empty character
Ancestry sat on their face
I conceive with study and toil
To dance the social staircase

To ride moxie's amend
Phoenix's recasting sword
To alien festering fears
Wake the dreams that snored

Old Photos

To the derelict summer of 1934
The rural feel of Washington State
To the tears of lifelong scarcity
And the fears of depression's fate

I see my grandma at twenty-four
Posed with Sunday dressed children
My young mother when only four
Grandma engendered three children

Threat of a fourth induced her
To a knitting needle's abort
She bled all though the moonlight
When heaven became her escort

My sorrow pales to this ordeal
Of the little children left behind
Without the love of their mother
Forever as tainted time

Monster Memories

Childhood's monster memories
Are character cousins that toll
It's the frantic in your fabric
And the burden of your soul

It's the time your got rejected
When your self-esteem took leave
You decided to become a wall
And learn to bob and deceive

It's the time your father failed you
When he cemented your distrust
He left you careened in the cold
And left your heart to rust

When your mother failed to rescue
And help when you fell down
That's when the pain pawned you
And made your existence a frown

Then your marriage took a mauling
It was your partner's fault, of course
Your heart is a product of the past
As your unconscious will endorse

Now you're a model of maturity
With the foundation of hindsight
To magazine monster memories
Into the wisdom of foresight

Playground Pivots

A return to all past playgrounds
    To character the innocent sounds

To evaluate the evasive evidence
    That play predicts benevolence

I time travel with memory's plight
    And time trigger with physical sight

I regress through a freedom of time
    To recall through a rogue of mine

Monkey bars and swings are rusty
    Yet, my memory is habit and husky

Images of fond friends and games
    Feelings of nostalgia not shame

I analyze each word and wrinkle
    Boy bonds are simple and fickle

Play is a pattern of progressions
    That abandons as life's aggressions

*Have you ever returned to the playgrounds of your
childhood to recapture the memories and lessons of youth,
to ponder how this influenced you the rest of life?*

The Color of Your Mind

For this reincarnation
I'm Caucasian for a while
I've learned lessons of creation
By running racial miles

I was stabbed on the schoolyard
And robbed on my paper route
I was beaten till unconscious
By Negro hate and doubt

The blood from childhood extends
To a creed of cruelty and colors
It flounders fair for me to revenge
The malice that fear discolored

Yet, I have no rage to return
Despite the scars that remain
I conceive their culture of burn
Like I've lived through their distain

All through my therapy salvations
I benefit and blossom the Black
When I dedicate my donations
It's colors that chug cognac

My peaceful paradox to exist
An uncanny umbrella to find
From a prior world I encrypt
Based on the color of your mind

Tiny Toddlers

Children thrive my sense of purpose
Emerging minds with heedful hearts
Like sharing a hot cup of Picasso
An internal warmth of abstract art

To volunteer with tiny toddlers
Delivers your heavenly dreams
Of making a decisive difference
With the sparkle of ego esteems

A transforming dream to glean
Completely alters your meaning
I can feel it serene my routine
And take my heart out for cleaning

If you're yet to be a parent
This wisdom gives you hands
It's your evolving era of merit
To springboard your life spans

*I'm thrilled to be a volunteer to tutor English and math to
disadvantaged kids. This piece was previously published in
an online magazine.*

First Steps

Delicate
steps and stumbles
when falling is an art
musical laugh and mumbles
the harmony of a child's
heart

Envy
time to tumble
I harbor your heartbeat
balance is your humble
until your feet are
fleet

Destiny
ripples to spawn
weaving waves of pride
genes that bounce beyond
from floor to savvy
guide

Tender
is a time of grace
and cuddling a right of way
baby girl with the sweetest face
steals my heart
away

*This is from watching my daughter first learn
to walk when she was 10 months old. It's a rare stage
when trial and error is bounce and laughs.*

Opium of the Orient

The liquid aroma of jasmine tea
   My bashful belly is warmed and free
      Colorful dragons are painting me
     The kung pao of my history

       Chop sticks and dim sum graces
        Childhood pockets of Cantonese
         The hospitality of Asian souls
         Cures fatigue with cultural ease

        Beijing duck and spicy shrimp
        Subtly sautéed in a wonder wok
      Magnetic moods of Hong Kong
      Cuisine of evolving social clocks

    Gourmet of radiant renditions
   Sunrises are spiced with tai chi
And campaigns of culinary cunning
Have timelessly transported me

*I'm thankful to be blessed with folkways based on harmony
and cooperation. This social style is much more
cooperative and humanistic than western societies.*

Childhood Capsules

Vexing childhood visions
Of men romancing men
Masquerading as women
Mavericks bending the trend

Forbidden are the females
With macho faces of stone
Flipping every faux pas
Morphing into clones

Sky high on the scaffolds
Daring dangles by a thread
Mannequins of marijuana
Laughing off their head

Downtown on the corners
Beggars brave a stand
Public chaos camping
Despair dares to expand

Glide Memorial Church
Weaving welfare wanderers
Meals and prayer and clothes
Ignored by elected conquerors

Trying to un-vex these visions
Of a scheme and skewer society
Its mediocrity for the marooned
And a spiral of social anxiety

Dragon Mother

Seeking a truthful embrace
Teen of explorative ways
Finally, I've been included
Sport with social praise

I beg for only a dollar
To play once a week
To carve a sense of belonging
A chance to be unique

Hitler, Hitler, Hitler
My mother shouts aloud
 Poverty's hate and fire
My spirits over plowed

My God I hate you so
Screaming ruptures my face
Gone in three more years
I'll kick you into space

Dagger of slicing rage
A cancer to bypass
Packed my mind before I die
Icy roads and shattered glass

Beggar at just fifteen
Wrestling loss of fate
Misandry her self-esteem
Dragon mothers born of hate

Group Home Groupies

When paltry change in your palm
Is less than a scrappy sandwich
Each night you finagle for food
Each day is an apple of anguish

Insight for who belongs
You access the authorities to allow
Too odious and old for adoption
A group home was endowed

You're a tangled teen of the time
Obscured in the occult of your own
You're bundled up in a package
To atone for future unknowns

Roommates are a renegade Russian
And a backstage boy from the Bronx
Your courage is daring to conform
And define the dimensions of the box

So goes my history in a hollow
Magazines of memoirs for the moths
Puzzles in life are capers of character
The future itself is a spicy sauce

Ghost Dad

Curiosity of a thirteen ager
A certificate of discovered birth
Like finding a severed hand
Crawling about the earth

I found my surname yet engaged
Mother recoiled like a snake
When inquired about my father
Claims her memory didn't take

When aligning my ancestry
I uncovered a sloppy note
Father always resided
Just eight miles down the road

She hid my father away from me
Black widows eat their mate
She left me standing on just one leg
And wore blinders to my fate

Mystery of 50 years ago
Ghost dad was just a noun
For this I killed my mother
And now she's underground

Poetic license allows one to unleash emotions in verse that one can't release in reality. It's really an expression of putting closure on life's lingering feelings in cathartic monologues.

Guest Poet

My uncle Lloyd Howard wrote these next two pieces in 1971. I included these because it's a window into his longing for his daughter. He felt he couldn't raise his daughter, so he gave full custody to her mom. But, the mother didn't want Lloyd to behave as her father and insisted that he remain only a friend when he visited. Worried that he wouldn't get to see his daughter, he agreed . "A Secret" and "My Little Girl" is the emotional fall out of this compromise.

A Secret

I know a secret place
A place I go now and then
I do what I want cause it's my world
Take my hand, come with me

Down into the dream world of my mind
Leave the cares of your world far behind
Take my hand, come with me

I will paint a vivid scene
And I'll sing a happy theme
It's my secret dream, come with me

But my dream is empty without you
Take my hand, please come with me

My Little Girl

I know a little girl
She's such a precious child
A little spoiled and very shy
But, who am I in her world?

Just barely six years old
A laughing happy child
But who am I in her world?
Just a friend of mommy's

When I go to visit
She's always glad to see me
But, she doesn't know how to treat me
She asks me if I've brought her
Any candy or a doll
Then she dashes out to play
Until its time to say
Goodbye to me

Yes, I know a little girl
She means the world to me
I love her so, it breaks my heart
Cause who am I in her world?
Just a friend of mommy's

In memory of Lloyd F. Howard (1932-1981)

Chapter Nine: Time and Age

The elusive concepts of time and age have intrigued people since the beginning. Probably because both are a loss of what we want to dearly hold onto. We may want to recapture what we feel we are losing in different ways. With this heightened awareness, it's natural that we react emotionally as we interpret these invisible and unstoppable forces. Join me while we muse on the meaning of time and age from different perspectives.

When you retire, social age is abandoned and you become the course of time.

Timeless Content

I Miss You

I miss tiptoeing in the morning
to silently sanction your slumber
and baking bread for breakfast
to perfectly habit your hunger

I miss waking you with warmth
to silently splendor your day
and getting you ready for school
to perfectly please your stray

I miss our weekends in the city
to silently culture your caper
and always kissing your forehead
to perfectly love and favor

I miss our evening dialogues
to silently stir your smarts
and embracing you everyday
to perfectly preserve your heart

After my daughter departed for college,
I realized that I would always miss her profoundly.

Photography

Fabrics of faces frozen in time
With the serenity of the shutter
A passage to magazine memories
Reversing life's closet of clutter

Junctures of effusive emotions
Mumbles from naked mankind
Unusual angles and exposures
The candor that time assigned

Panorama of your paradox past
How you aged within the maze
Lost emotions dripping the floor
Your archive of gripping essays

A chronicle of moving existence
Old passports for you to discern
Character maps of perplexity
From the lessons of life's return

The Art of Aging

You're the age of altered aging
As a vintage of solar sphere
It's a purview of perspective
As destiny to memory's years

It's your passage for forgiveness
As maturity's final face lift
It's the gunpowder of purpose
As meaning soothes your drift

It's your heart ebbing emotions
As your body comes to term
It's the harmony of thought
As the clever will discern

Aging is relative to art
As perspective is relative to balance

Ancestry

Adventurer's journey of doubt
Searching for truth and being
Curiosity and nostalgia to tout

Great time of lingering last
Faces and dreams, lost and dashed
Unearth the legends of past

Decrepit photos past their prime
To examine, to infer, to muse
Clandestine clues of ancient time

Peer deep into their face and eyes
Map of wrinkles your answer lies
Of tragic lows and romantic highs

Span the bridge of floating clan
Boats only embrace or evade
Glean your sagas quick you can

Sequels parade while memories frayed
Chronicle to ponder life's intent
Legacy you are to destiny yet made

College Daughter

Delivered as you departed
My heart is dripping pride
Your talking eyes are artist
And your mind is amplified

Ascendancy is laughter
College jumps a stride
You're the creator hereafter
Of futures surfing the tide

Now my thoughts collide
Your imprinted image of mine
Stretching to smile inside
Yet feelings twist and grind

To digest another phase
My gut turned upside down
Missing your spirited ways
Memories tease my frown

When I'm inclined to dine
Your essence thrives with me
Emptiness looking to find
I imagine you perfectly

How graceful of you to chat
Silence to those less free
In sync like acrobats
Breathing vicariously

Rhythms Without Beats

Last chatter long ago
Request to borrow money
Best friends do bestow
A bridge until it's sunny

A faux pas that silenced our chime
Joy and laughter gone astray
Ravages of age and time
A dear friend has slipped away

Discovered in cyberspace
Until I read the script
Our connection is erased
A memorial for his crypt

Twisted for twenty years
A blindness that alienates
Climate of beer and cheers
Farewell my star roommate

His life was stop and stumble
Yet found his heavenly slice
A luscious green jungle
Of earthly paradise

Petty thoughts are quirk
Rogue rhythms without beats
Nostalgia's parting smirk
My life circle incomplete

In memory of my friend and best roommate
Lishus Husband 1943-2014; I miss your laughter.

———

Shapeless Time

Segments of mosaic reality
Aging has altered my time
To savor pinnacle pieces
Squander nothing sublime

The terror of expiring worlds
Shock waves rattle my spine
Future of temporal uncertainty
Cyclones sweeping my mind

Distractions rob the senses
Electronics hasten the pace
Capture timeless memories
The prisoners of embrace

Rites of passage of eras
Sand slipping through rhymes
Flow of waning motion
Winter of shapeless times

When you're retired, time takes on a shapeless form as your orientation and priorities change. The cycles of the clock and sun no longer matter as time recast itself into thought and movement.

Triggers of the Train

The blaring baritone, a barnacle train
Triggers echoes of memory's champagne
Meanders the mind, journeys of play
Of nostalgic and nomadic edgeways

Childhood embraces, fossilized faces
Telltale teasing aloft of arms graces
A mushroom montage, vogue notions attract
Time released themes of rogue artifacts

All the laughs and fears, loves and tears
Are roaring away as melodic lost years
This daily trigger refines my domain
The blaring baritone of the barnacle train

Your Second Act

Melodies that mingle, your concerto everyday
Tasking is the rhythm to aspire your ballet
Patterns of the past, our challenge to decant
Framing self-esteem is our nature to enchant

Graduating phases, a puzzling game plan
The future is the epic of your evolving lifespan
Setting goals of fate, like chasing streetcars
Moving compositions to catch for memoirs

Stop phantom fear, find your inner guru
Second acts beckon for thoughts of the few
Timing is your gauge, intent is your leapfrog
Celebrated theater is your drama's epilogue

Rites of Passage

What exactly are the rites of passage?
Antiquities of rituals for the savage
From cultures that dictate each curve
To venues that cultivate each swerve

From those who routine life missions
To those robots of typecast transitions
Rabble your role and mold your mask
Your paradox path is tradition of task

If you agree to export your destiny
You invert your security of identity
So we parody with two hearts in our hollow
One for society and one to free follow

Time of Your Life

Was it the whimsical wonder?
Of a childhood fantasy quest
Love and nurturing mother
Where depth of emotions crest

Was it voltage of the mind
The electricity of college daze
The freedom of cerebral design
Swagger the scholarly maze

Was it the zeal of success
Climbing a career with wits
Celebrate savvy and finesse
Security of purpose and glitz

Was it a duet of passion
A partner worthy of love
Where marriage is your fashion
To ascend as joyful doves

Was it unconditional love
Spawning the next generation
Magic of nourishing gloves
Pride of lifelong creation

Was it exotic vacations
To amazing times and places
Of seductive aspirations
Enticing cultural embraces

Was definition your strife?
Seize every day to expand
Shift the meaning of life
Let your bucket list command

Misfits of Fears

Jugglers riding storms
Bodies tumbling through time
Wrestling with the wind
Twisting without a spine

Undressed of social graces
Forever friends of life
Regressions and betrayals
Victims of their own device

Compelled to cocoon
In liquids of shrinking minds
Drips creeping fragility
Of paranoid mankind

Dwindling life squandered
Bunker mentality of time
Epochs lost to hiding
Yet intruders are undefined

Anxiety erodes longevity
Goodbye misfits of fears
Annoying to remember
In my reflective years

This is a response to my life long friends who are
stumbling into old age with uncertainty and trepidation.

In Light of Gray

Musing in the mirror
   Grayness I must tear
      Wrinkles map my frown
         Burden, truth and scare

Glimpse deep into optics
   Craters of pensive size
      Cerebral art of colors
         The scholar is still wise

Time is drowning quickly
   Spellbound with phantom land
      Until you capture your stroke
         Your mind is just quicksand

Farewell to ties of time
   Greetings to destiny vast
      Balloons of pupils swell
         Drums of heart recast

Finally you breathe a vision
   Your stunning spell has spun
      Your steak has popped and sizzled
         And dreams of Eden begun

Seize the light of gray
   Tribute family and friend
      Purpose lingering passions
         Legacy's fashion to send

Life Review

To a life of novel revelations
Historically fresh insights
Mutations of timeless memories
In the motions of past birthrights

Your personal rhapsody
That characters each citation
An unconscious need to rejoice
Enshrining the bonds of salvation

If burden is the weight of review
And confusion the cloud of events
Let recasting simplify the script
Of emotional discontents

From surfing nature's antiquity
To the venture freedoms astound
From the love and tears entwined
To destiny's proving ground

With ancestral continuity
Your expiring patterns to contrast
The epilogue of life is closure
With an eye to the next forecast

The graduation of your time to space

Born Without a Birthday

My best friend is odd
Montage from the start
A feeling life is flawed
Of people without hearts

Lifestyle of a loner
Who bonds with very few
Schizophrenic mother
Who rendered him askew

Frequent fall and fumble
Bungled each life stage
Insights from his puzzle
His folly refines my gauge

Invisible burden so long
Homeless with Descartes
His existential song
A saving grace of smarts

A mental pub crawl
Our conversations are wit
We soar above the banal
Of scholarly hypocrites

Tears for my fallen friend
Grim reaper swept his way
I hope his soul finds refuge
Born without a birthday

*In memory of my friend and roommate, Nikita Hoyer
(1940-2014). I miss our winding walks and twisted talks.*

Retirement Dreams

Bestowed with a youthful body
Mentored by a magazine mind
Now drama is time's odyssey

As you question your questions
And you doubt your doubts
You are enigma's impression

Fascinated by freedom's ease
Tempered by novel transitions
Bliss is learning your breeze

A wealth of adjustment spins
In fantasy flies your future
Your dawn of design begins

Horizons of hypnotic hope
Themes of ignited intent
The id to your future scope

To ménage your memory's lore
Restyle your social swagger
Unlock your heart's back door

Our Eternal Soul

Biological entity
Shelf life beyond the self
Boasting its own identity
Morality's immortal elf

Soul of life's meaning
Of all my other pasts
History's infinite weaning
Ancestral wisdom recast

Surfing your timeless esprit
Is my mind part of you
Or is your keenness part of me?
And are we truly free?

Shapeless plasma form
A known energy ghost
Anguish or brainstorm
Glad I'm your current host

There is no coffin to fear
Since soul lives beyond
And travels in a sphere
Until its time to spawn

Dream of eternal appeal
Dance and laugh with death
Feeling alive and surreal
Past my final breath

*My science prevented my belief in the soul until I started
reading accounts of those who passed and returned.*

My Frayed Face

Movements
Quick and swift
My cinema of mental clarity
Parting the wind is a drift
With youth of
dexterity

My eyes
Follow her trace
My image can't respond
Her pace has frayed my face
And bunked my body
beyond

She freezes
Me with her breeze
My feet have grown to stone
Slow motion is my tease
She dashes my
time zones

My daughter
Was under a wing
When taught soccer's delight
She tangles now my strings
And collects her
birthright

*A time comes to all parents where your child grows up
and surpasses you on a physical and mental plane.*

Just Smile

My extraordinary daughter
Time has come to pass the torch to you
Smart, determined and loyal--Just Smile

Don't worry for me my dear, do not shed a tear
I had a wild and wonderful time
A romantic hippie of the years—Just Smile

Our time in sync was love and play
Our era was sport, travel and laughs
Childhood was our sacred ballet—Just Smile

I love teaching you to read at two
Fixing lunch and walking you to school
Then playing ball or swimming the pool--Just Smile

Our love continues past heaven's gate
Who knew we'd be soul mates
My pride, my joy and best of fate—Just smile

I guess I have to fly goodbye
But, no matter where I have to flee
I'll save your place right next to me --Just Smile

When I think of you, I always smile
So, when your mind swirls of me
My parting wish for you is--Just Smile

———

People of Chance

People of chance who drifted away
Insights engage at a ripe age
The tally of adventure is hindsight
As we evolve into our sage

To the blinders of a busy hustle
Entanglements are my forever
To magnetic social meaning
When folly is so clever

Romances damper and dissolve
Savory slices of heavenly cake
Gracing upon our paltry plates
Fantasies of lost namesakes

Vast friendships of mutual respect
Longing to endure a lifetime
Now shelved like a dusty book
A faux pas sans reason or rhyme

This disconnected vagueness
Are lost mates of the archetype
I vow to humane each one again
From the shadows of stereotype

Flowers from Heaven

Headlines of the day healed my heart
Blessings for Bailey and her bouquet
A divine delivery from her dad
With a card on her 21st birthday

He hovers in heaven for five years
Retired early from a caper of cancer
She was barely sixteen and careened
A hobbled heart without an answer

The annual flowers dawn bright colors
He scribes her as the jewel of his life
He'll always love and be with her
She just needs to look into the light

Pre-paid flowers before he departed
He lavished love in all his cards
Hearts transcend time and place
Forever's rapture of radiant regards

What a heartfelt way to remember and thank those who
were so important in our lives. Imagine the eternal
emotion of receiving a gift from a departed loved one.

Sixty-Five Years

Today is my sixty fifth birthday
Raining with raging reflections
The mind still grills like a gourmet
While the body bellows objections

My feet have faded fleetness
These eyes wade weary too soon
Spices chase my stomach to recess
And my libido leaped in a cocoon

Par for the course is perplexity
Milestones of meaning to endorse
Fifteen more years of life expectancy
Dancing on destiny's doors

I'm charmed to have the return
Of lusty girlfriends of the past
Only the moonlight can discern
Despite relationships amassed

So I embrace these earthly miracles
Of beautiful people and paradise places
With a wandering now so whimsical
To embody lost memory traces

19 Candles

Cuddling her with curry cuisine
Hand picked Haight-Ashbury gifts
And candles on chocolate muffins
For my daughters birthday drift

She is a moving mosaic of mime
Recasting to the calling of college
To rejoice with minds of friends
And sculpt a character of knowledge

My eyes are awry saying goodbye
When your heart is going away
No matter how painted with pride
She is my sweet and sole bouquet

Resolved to savor museum moments
When eyes echo and words woo
With the gift of epoch embraces
My memory will forever accrue

Happy Birthday

The After Bucket List

A connection of mind and matter
      Beyond what the future can gather
            Earthly goals to garner and close
                  Timelines to preserve like prose

If you sensed and studied the soul
      You crave revival's console
            Cellular energy resumes the ride
                Each century is a memory's guide

The joy of returning to old haunts
      And hanging with past friends I flaunt
            To run the final of the Olympic mile
                And catch a Super Bowl score in style

To explore our secret base on Mars
      And break bread with people of stars
            But, if you think I'm a tad unlaced
                What's your next DESTINY in space?

Statue of Dreams

To sum up your dreams before the curtains fall
To scribe a sprawling verse as your port of call

Your freedom is deprived if taken by surprise
Or wait for others to describe you in their cries

We carry on so misunderstood and impromptu
Families eulogize through a narrow construe

Rarely stop to think how we want to be inked
As your mind and soul move more distinct

Is all we've done here the sum of our sphere?
We sacrifice for crawlers throughout the years

Our legacy of time is our language of love
Our inner design is our pride from above

Human lives can be limitless, yet this is so confined
Smiling eyes, our passion and hopes all left behind

Our wishes may thrive as statues of dreams
Our memory may survive as words of esteems

Transitions

From infant to infinity
Your emerging cyclone of cells
Is passing through your walls
Like a storm of gusty gazelles

Many costumes of childhood
Of innocence and insecurity
A passage of time dependence
To nature's uncertainty

The tangled mind of a teen
A cauldron of maze and mire
Survival of turbulent tempers
Depends on intrepid desire

Labor is the curse of adulthood
Talent is the measure of themes
With constantly changing angles
Creativity needs clever schemes

In the organic notion of offspring
Parenthood can rise and shine
Your transition outside yourself
Is your future of genetic design

Self-esteem finally settles
After you're groovy and gray
Waiting is another transition
A camouflage for yesterday

Release Me

I can view when horizons are done
And view where guide spirits begun

I hear their final thoughts as chimes
And hear their fading laugh of times

I feel the drown of a falling sun
And feel my heart as fading done

I smell the end of each birthday
And broken history held at bay

I know the secret of heaven's embrace
And know not to worry or lose face

I sense a craving for time of peace
And sense a longing to be released

Chapter Ten: Biography Bounces

The chapter on Biographical Poems is intended to bring a revelation, epiphany, insight or a fresh interpretation of this character to the reader from fresh and unusual angles.

Sharp edges of granite faces
shredding minds of time
are cleft in their paces
of eternal parting chimes.

Content of Characters

I Am Frankenstein

I am a frightened toddler running from demons
that I made up in my head.
I am the dark shadow of a missing character
that is tricking the deathbed.
I turn the corner of poverty into emptiness
that a step-child feels with dread.

I am a broken window's mind seeking
the answer to all of mankind.
I am the visions of future social missions
for the chronically disinclined.
I am the memory of passing dire ships
for cargos that malign.

I am the birth of a day without sun
and a mother's voice of guns.
I am the tainted trunk of a winter's tree
that the midnight shuns.
I am Frankenstein with scissors of emotions
until I love someone.

Femmes of Fashion

I admire the fashion of city women
Where art and self-esteem cross
The attention to detail of delivery
Is their language of social sauce

London, Paris and New York
Karan, Armani and Coco Chanel
A swagger supplied by superstars
For a feeling of a flying gazelle

Manikin models get all the mojo
Maps of male styles rarely revise
The visage of exclusive vogues
Is the drama of designs in disguise

I'm beckoned by the billow of beauty
And so jealous of the creation of chic
The artistry and intrigue of fashion
Is to parlay physique with mystique

Pregnancy Paradise

When your hormones are howling
And your stomach is swirling
Strange cravings are cultivated
While emotions are churning

Whispers and waggles from within
That melts your heart devout
A child conceived is a ceremony
Of destiny's love beyond doubt

Ramble the road of genetic genius
Garden the fruits of coexistence
You're the magic moms of miracles
And the legacy of existence

Motherhood

Reiko and Dorothy

Two little school girls of only six
    Holding hands, wearing wild flowers
        The cocoon of early life is a drift
            When best friends are passing the hours

Bombs from Japan came as a jolt
    Countries combusted with fear
        Girls were punished if they played
            The innocent crying to cohere

Dorothy was willing to disguise
    She smuggled over to romp and revel
        Shunned and severed was poor Reiko
        A friend, a risk, and not the devil

Hark the herding of families begin
    The school skipped a good-bye party
        Flows and festers of fears and tears
            Teachers never said they were sorry

Now your life is what you can carry
    Locked and barbed in a one room shack
        In a swamp of despair to survive
            Forever plagued with these flashbacks

Seventy-five years later burns the flame
    Dorothy's find was timely and traced
        Reiko's dream had finally come true
        Smiling souls are eternally embraced

*After 75 years, these best friends had an emotional
reunion. Reiko who just wanted to say "Thank you for
being my friend when everyone else was mean."*

Lightning Lindsey

She is pure
Child of the earth
Future of a pale planet
Unraveling infinity at birth

Her eyes smile
Climbing vines of visions
Curious critiques of thought
On the history of idle decisions

Hungry genes
Freight train personality
Archetypes of exploration
Evolving the social morality

Rising yeast of youth
Undaunted by this odyssey
Voltage vows of rebel radiance
The calculus of organic ecology

Standing on novel ideals
Pushing on relic traditions
This culture that's frozen in time
Sparks lightning of her ambition

Notes from Heaven

In the news is the story of Elena
Whose heart was cascading with love
A cute six-year old girl with cancer
Who left gifts for her parental doves

She scribed a litany of love letters
She hid in drawers, socks and books
And graced her dad a last dance
Despite her terminal outlook

Three years have passed to this day
Doves still discover darling notes
She liked to draw and spell backwards
After time had taken her throat

Each note rips mom's heart anew
Her ecstasy to agony unending
Until she finally realized the code
It's hugs and kisses she's sending

*They say Elena "found grace even in the smallest details"
of life and was smiling until the end. Her parents wrote a
book based on her unique story called Notes Left Behind.*

Sleeping Man

There is a sleeping man
In his borrowed clothes
Holding on so tight
To a wilted rose

Face of old leather
Mapped with many roads
Dark and circled eyes
Scars of lost abodes

Life is full of rivals
There's everyday to tame
Society of survival
Panhandle is his game

There is a young lady
Occasionally with a smile
They have a little chat
Brevity is her style

She brings a single flower
He brightens like a star
Then dies as she departs
Perhaps a daughter's scar

I know this fallen person
I put money in his hand
I rarely say a word
There is a sleeping man

*This was my premiere poem that published when I
first started writing in my second act.*

Belated Biography

Do you miss paradox people
  And wonder of relationships past
   Of unique encaged personalities
     Young curiosity didn't forecast?

     Memory muses of seventh grade
       Idle images of a faded friend
         Waves of warmth from smiling eyes
           He brightened my dark like godsend

           Bestowed a school biography
           His architecture is my appeal
           To reconstruct his past particles
           And naively trigger the surreal

           His mother minted a warping scar
           A shot in the head during a pall
           He was sitting in the next room
           And saw gray matter splash the wall

         My heart now flopped to the floor
         With sorrow shaking my bones
         I reached inside my friend's mind
         And forever cried as his clone

     His presence precludes an existence
     To a hospital hollow to bereave
     My heart is bleeding to tell him
     In my dear friend, I'll always believe

   *My friend returned to a mental hospital for depression
     shortly after this and I never saw him again.*

The Actor

Eyes of blue that bankrupt
The chiseled face of veracity
A moving style of an epoch era
The narcissism of audacity

My patient losing his purpose
Of dealing with dire delays
Of acting on the abnormal
Rogue rhythms of everyday

He drank the elixir of an extra
Twenty years renown and removed
Star gazing begs to gamble
Hoping your sight is renewed

Cliffhanging on fraying fingers
Is slowly marooning the mind
Into a room of delirious dreams
And a reality the devil defined

My patient did one commercial 24 years
ago and is still waiting for a return call.

Birthday Book

To be forever cuddly, forever cute
Of memory's love, of bearing fruit

To notes of nostalgia, to nesting outlooks
Of historic content, of birthday books

To chronicles of costumes, to times of candor
Of days and moments, of majestic meander

To dashing details, too dashing to dismiss
Of dreamy lips, of a soul mate's kiss

To photos of years, to tears of persistence
Of maturity's map, of roads of existence

To values to vault, to values to venture
Of my fading away, of times adventure

To be your annual, to be an animation
Of your special day, of my adoration

To perks of heaven, to you a mystique
Of hugs and kisses, of keen to your cheek

When we created my daughter's birthday book,
I promise to celebrate its progression by being
present at all her birthdays, even when I'm gone.

Black in America

To grow up outside looking in
To feel the world's melodic motion
As passing waves of whispered wishes
Floating endlessly in an ocean

I grasp for these phantom dreams
Indulging my identity to depend
On the outcome of social slants
And my prayers that apprehend

Knocking on life's glass door
My conquered cries go unheard
I surrender my self and soul
Into and reality still deferred

Adulthood is less than dreams believe
And beyond the trap that's hostile
Existence doesn't belong to me
Only sulking shadows of exile

A common goal of both the therapist and poet is to get outside yourself to become another identity, time, or reality.

Sonnet for Shakespeare

Childhood mystery so sketchy and scant

Wed at eighteen, three children to enchant

Began an actor, playwright to traverse

A true bard in his heart, wrote stage as verse

Obsessive with meter much less with rhyme

Loved time and beauty like O mistress mine

Mastered comedies and tragedies for vogue

"To be or not to be" famous question of old

Sonnets of obsessive love to a young man

Lust for dark ladies, critics can't understand

Both punished with death as medieval rule

Quill of libido his fantasy of fuel

A Poet's etchings bare character revealed

Healing expressions while infamy is sealed

Steve Jobs

Fire in his eyes
Given away at birth
Set a disposition
He never could reverse

Reject the status quo
Rebel is his heart
Of past hyped minds
A hippie of Descartes

Amazing future vision
Pushing the human race
Forward so he famed
On just an interface

Distrust and scorn of people
Understood by few
Anger whips rejection
While boosting his value

Touch of social charisma
Eased his personal pain
Lifestyle of simplicity
Perfection bought campaign

Innovator of minds
Discoveries are profound
Yet rebelled with health
Suspicion wears a frown

Aero Earhart

Scrawny Kansas girl
Wanderlust driven core
Nurse and social worker
Empathy for the war

Kept scrapbooks pristine
Eclipsing famous men
Of successful heroines
Equality's new bullpen

Her true romance of freedom
Gliding through the air
In all three dimensions
A soul mate beyond the rare

Her challenge is her passion
Bravery takes a degree
Breaking male barriers
A harbinger soaring free

Daredevil's celebrity status
Even a line of clothes
Proved her point beyond
By risking life and prose

"Marriage is just a cage"
Her heart is a burning rogue
Free thinker before her time
Creates a lasting vogue

Einstein's Music

He often thought in music
    Defining his life and dreams
        Rhythms for his mind
            Springboard for extremes

        Patterns of split harmony
            Structure of new thought
                Framework for equations
                An evolving juggernaut

            Passion for novel ideas
              Crossroads of space and time
              Travel the speed of light
              Your age will never climb

              Universe is expanding
              With curvatures of space
              Watch for waves of gravity
            And light particles in your face

           From atoms to wormholes
         Threatening ideas astound
        Fleeing Nazi barbarity
      Yet America style confounds

      In racism, he saw a disease
      Risking to speak aloud
    Bounty placed on his head
Proud music from his cloud

Sigmund Freud

Looking for answers
  To the puzzles of life
    Searching old masters
      Where insight curbs strife

To see through the mind
  Theory changes thought
    Hypnosis of formulas
      Shrinking the distraught

Locked hidden memories
  Unconscious is key
    Queuing our behavior
      You thought you were free

One symbol at a time
  Personal depth of meaning
    Summation of the rhyme
      Which character is leaning

Victorian driven matrix
  A legacy needing keys
    Original theories predict
      Concepts on a trapeze

In his personal nest
  Love and lust collide
    Angst of his own repressions
      His duel character divide

Maria Curie

Most famous female scientist
Obscured from what we know
Hatched in Polish Russia
To rainbows of skid row

At ten, her closest sister dusted
Too soon her mother hollowed
A dysphoric webs of loss
Lifelong demons followed

Refuge in academia
Bled and bargained for school
Two times the Nobel Prize
New chemistry and physics rules

Radiation cures mutations
Her future demise of cancer
Yet, mobbed for upstaging men
Misogyny cloaked dancer

Passion of raising mankind
Braved x-rays to the battlefield
Million men were treated
Yet, scorned by those she healed

Eternal passion for science
Honest and humble flower
Welcomed death as a relief
From hate of inferior cowards

Cleopatra VII

Named for father's glory
    Ancestry's offer of power
Nine languages and philosophy
    Wit and clout's shower

Queen of empty Egypt
    Eighteen years yet rules
Must marry little brother
    Govern together as tools

Discord created a rift
    Male dominance iron grip
Shaped against themselves
    Maneuvers into crypt

Finesse Caesar's heart
    To defend her crown to shrills
Ally the Roman Empire
    From crafty political skills

Mark Antony won her heart
    Power and children charms
Romance of the ages
    Until he died in her arms

Crushed, she took her life
    And left a quote for the wise
"All strange and terrible events welcome,
    but comforts we despise"

Mother Teresa

Agnes of Macedonia
Lost her father at eight
Catholic mother guides
Life of charity creates

School a rigid convent
Forced religious life
Became a teenage nun
Despite internal strife

Crisis of personal faith
Frustrations empty and dark
Gospel fails poverty people
She designed her own ark

Intervention in India
Shaped this break of heart
Suffering so rampant
Health clinics shine smart

Sacrificed the needs of the self
To ignite the empathy that rages
Forgoing marriage and children
For a higher calling of sages

Explodes an enduring passion
A stunning legacy ensures
Remedies in a hundred countries
Her Nobel Prize of cures

Mozart's Tempo

Gift of melodic ears
Coddled in maestro arms
Wrote music before words
Memory pristine that charms

Composing works at five
Symphony fate at eight
Father paraded him proud
Concerto of ego ornate

Work is a ship without sails
Pieces of wax and wane
Feudalism that prevails
A servant's ball and chain

Pursuit of free expression
Roaming poverty years
Vienna overture begins
Two children for his tears

Scholars remain confused
Fecal erotic trends
Virtuoso of his pen
Curve of character bends

Six hundred musical gifts
Yet, broke at thirty-five
Suddenly ill and depressed
Departed, his spirit deprived

Tenacious Tesla

Walked ten miles a day
Fed the pigeons at every turn
Brainstormed with the moonlight
A passion never adjourned

The mind of a laboratory
Travel, concepts, and schematics
Pride of electrical glory
Genius of mechanical dynamics

He refused a wife and children
A ripping emotional distraction
To save creative juices
For visions of future abstractions

Speechless and confounded
Were the scientists of the day
Gifted voltage free to all
But, greed would choke and decay

Unschooled and angry Edison
Sabotaged him from behind
Marconi stole the Nobel
On Tesla's radio design

Government swiped his work
When he died poor and alone
Textbooks buried him as quirk
His genes I hope we clone

*Albert Einstein was once asked what its like being
the smartest man in the world. He said that he wouldn't
know and to ask Nikola Tesla instead.*

Dixie Gypsy

Renditions of feminine men
With hair made of wheat
Masculine are the femmes
With faces of concrete

Rogues of fragmented reality
In the humble heart of Dixie
On the fringe of a fading existence
Whispers the wandering gypsy

Their camps are ill at ease
Deaf children of squalor charm
Swing the trapeze of survival
Reaching for life without arms

Invisible people are frail
Peer deep into their eyes
This dullness and apathy
Are characters burglarized

Born askew are random orphans
Cult capsules don't foreclose
Life is a memory of déja vu
Sulking in shifting shadows

Entitlement completely erased
Replaced by faceless fear
This obscurity is an embrace
For identity to disappear

Make My Day

The morning motions of winter weather
I startled a woman made of leather

Her hands and body wrapped in yardage
Grueling through the gloomy garbage

Worn and dreary these dark eyes
With fragile face of stormy skies

"Hello, will bottles help your cause?"
"Thank you not, glass cuts my paws"

A virtuous voice so precise and polite
A hobbled heart so forlorn and finite

In wealthy waters, hunger still expands
Into a poverty of drowning life spans

Integrity forbids you to ignore
And gyrates my empathy to the core

Aptly bestowed to make her day
Funds and hugs are my best convey

*Homelessness has its biography in every city I've resided
in going back to childhood. It's in Seattle, San Francisco,
Los Angeles, and even Phoenix. It's become an common
backdrop for the modern society in America.*

Two Hearts Live Twice

Face of a beaten baseball glove
Green eyes of a murky swamp
Vocal chorus without true tones
To a cigarette he loves to chomp

Boasting inmate blues and bluster
A depth of pride for the prison proud
Falling to knees and grabbing his chest
Surrounded by the smoke of his shroud

A mouse in the medical maze
Seeking a partner to dance
Doctor decreed a human heart
Luck on the wings of chance

Stanford surgery gave him swagger
Celebrity's first million dollar inmate
He returned to prison with puffy pride
And tailored traits of a new birth date

So rare to clone a second self
A rebirth without a pause or price
He sustained his sequel of smoking
And claimed he got to live twice

*This inmate who received a heart transplant, but he
continued his chain smoking habit and passed away less
than a year later at the age of 32. He will forever be
known as the "million dollar inmate."*

The Affected Artist

Saucy sketches seduce my mind
Before my eyes engage the edges
Floating figures and inverted images
Parade to display their pledges

Rummaging in this random vain
My imaginary matrix morning
On canopies of fugitive design
Are frescos of ideas forming

I grind my pigments into paste
And painstakingly ease the plaster
I beckon and fate my brushes
And trace the draft of my master

With gastric juices in my hands
Every tint is a testimony of mine
Each stroke is a saint of patience
Each theme is a tease of time

Soft solo is the painter's soul
To be unique and undaunted each day
Is swimming in waning waters
As the perils of life's portray

Woman's Advocate

The fabric of a female advocate
Is striving to shed your skin
Becoming your raw emotions
To think like a woman's twin

> Can you be a role reversal?
> Risk your feelings on your sleeve
> Prioritize relationships with people
> And embrace contagion to conceive

Endure pennies for hours long of work
Model marriage as fame and fashion
While domestic duties entail
Self-sacrifice as proof of passion

> With love and longevity echoes
> And procreation heaven bestows
> Genetic selection is self-designed
> To create a race of cast and flow

I'm honored to be a woman's advocate by authoring
Creative Retirement for Women. I now realized how bias
and stereotyped a modern society is toward women and
the amount of work that still needs to be done.
Carpe Diem

The Pensive Poet

Swimming in the mire of memories
Nostalgia enraging bare bones
Angles of agony pressing my skin
A vision that vaults life's tone

Each day I sunrise my mind
A vortex of ideas to engage
Petty perceptions asking to renew
Concepts competing for the stage

I strive to scheme under my skin
To question each sense of serenity
To fractal all hidden feelings
And compel an inverted identity

An imposter within myself
Entangled by irrational esteems
Where verse is the only venue
And escape occurs only in dreams

Hippie Hamlet

To canopy cohorts, to sparkling stars
    Of parks of pardons and sleeping memoirs

To spawning trees, to hippie harvest
    Of flowing through to artery gardens

To emerald pastures, to misty cities
    Of social vows of igniting the sixties

To liquid music, to tempo and tease
    Of personal insight of humanity's keys

To toil for truth, to toil for love
    Of integrity and wit of peace thereof

To change the course, to change the time
    Of mankind's prejudice to a new paradigm

Yes, I'm a relic from the 1960s who grew up in the cultural movement in San Francisco's Haight Ashbury. These liberal social ideals have forever guided my life and partitioned my personality.

Queen of England

My eyes are fuel, are macho machines
Undoing the sheen, the reptile queen

Reality is a slice, is rolling the dice
Part human, part animal, part twice

Scales of green, scales of dismay
Witnesses of integrity of her betray

To fear the shadows, to fear the self
Hidden world leaders in refuge on shelves

She aptly apologizes; she's half and half
Claims you'll still love her, she laughs

Not rogue reality, not for rogue me
All stem leaders are stems of this tree

*When it came out that the queen is reptilian, her website
offered an apology and attempt to allay any fears. She
admitted she was not completely human, but said she loves
all her subjects anyway.*

Pirate President

Hoax the election, based on fears
The voting public's line coheres
Gastric juices, irrational thought
Where lurid lies love blind spots

Jealous politics, marbled with hate
Form the fear of those who immigrate
All the social problems, made as planned
Say you're the savior, they melt in your hand

To build a wall, box out your dreary
Hide in a hole and be a peeping leery
Foil the food rations, if poor or feeble
Starve the same sheep that clothed you evil

Reverse all the cures, use the back door
Contrive the tax code so the sheep pay more
Pathological liars, republican armies
Bullies of power and money parties

Darkness fills the days, lightness loses time
A ruling sociopath unable to reason or rhyme
Self defeating ignorance, American herds
I'd love to flee the country like a free bird

Chapter 11: Quicksand Quotes

Many of these quotes and aphorisms are lines that have gone rogue to their original purpose. Their intentions and dimensions have not been compromised as they have found their way to expression. You will find various love, existential and retirement quotes since these are the major themes in my time line.

Employment is just a social reflection weaving our minds into mirrors of time.

Love Quotes

1   Romantic love often ends when awareness begins
of differences hoping to blend.

2   Love is the sanctuary of a meandering mind
and the therapist of heedful heart.

3   Love does not set you free; it captures you into
the emotional expression of your history.

4   Escaped embraces and floating faces
scheme dream identities from romantic spaces.

5   The psychology of attraction is controlled
by childhood traits undiscovered within the self.

6   Love is a trance, a whimsical chance
when scanning ships meet sensual glance.

7   If we can only mitigate each others personal flaws,
Love's kinship of a lifetime shines with ego applause.

8   Romance is full of laughter or hurts me till I cry,
a storm of southern comfort or kisses from the sky.

9   Your inner child's love is innocence and
Broadway, novel naiveté on a stage of social display.

10   When love is a liquid being, its genius is
congealing the fluids of nomad feelings.

11   Love doesn't find you if your lost,
it follows you into the memory of caretakers.

12   Your emotional identity is a combination
of the character of all prior loves.

13   The insight of love will patiently linger for the
darkness to empty and the dawn to discern.

14   Legendary love is the fashion model
of impressions on your heart's dauntless dreams.

15   Minding the heart is mending the mind
of heartless minds of love.

16   If marriage is the root of love's clout,
uniqueness is the facade of simple doubt.

17   To costume love's spell is a masquerade
for theatrical fools of the trade.

18   The ecstasy of envy kisses
unhinges me into excesses
where fantasy never sleeps.

19   Women are the biological curators of existence
and the emotional path of least resistance.

20   A child conceived is a ceremony of confidence
beyond the mind's destiny of doubt.

21   Your facial fractures that flash before seen
seduces the savvy to read your genes.

22   The impulse of unconscious seeking
stems from a heart of hidden traits.

23   Intelligent love redesigns fabled freedoms
to shelter and sage unique personalities.

24   The pungent aroma of a broken heart
is creative energy for my next Bogart.

25   Loves conveyed and contrived from another time
are empire lessons for future designs.

26   Love is the music of a hidden harmony
and the lyrics of a balance beam.

27   The range of romance is a code of camouflage
obliged to musings and mirage.

28   The blazing flames of infatuation
kindles the thoughtful tempers of the mind.

29   Computer dating is handing over your heart
to a machine that doesn't give a damn.

30   If you are seduced by memories past,
your transgressions are a need for closure.

31   The lyrical keys to your heart
are the melodies from prior love rhythms.

32   I engage my relationships as if I am at the
crossroads of nature and evolution.

*33 If you allow your heart to sail your ship,
the maestro of passion determines kinship.*

*34 We fall in love with parental images
to nurture a neglected inner child.*

Existential Quotes

*1 Life is crying into the sun,
so I make rainbows.*

*2 It's a folly to fight to fit in
when legend is meant to stand out.*

*3 Freedom is a liquidity of thought
while democracy is the solidity of behavior.*

*4 Waiting for life's wake up call only extends
the slumber of a disguised existence.*

*5 Flying without wings enjoys not
without a yen to roam.*

*6 Existence that precedes essence
is an insult to your soul.*

*7 The best predictor of future behavior
is always past behavior.*

*8 If we are really condemned to be free, then we are
free to un-condemn and redefine our existence.*

9   Rebelling from cultural cocaines
is the vigor of identity's venture.

10   Social absurdity in our existence
is a passing breeze of a neurotic character.

11   Your lifespan is your identity
divided by time and space. $L = i / t+s$

12   Creating destiny's vision is the ghosted
genetics of an expanding humanity.

13   Your creativity expires to encore
while craving fragments for fate to explore.

14   Society's symbolic images and meanings
are balls and chains of archaic beings.

15   An erupting existence craves character mutation
as salvation for the alter ego.

16   Labor of love that hesitates
bleeds each and every day.

17   Vogue ideas are rogue Van Gogh.

18   The determinations of thought are the particles
of energy and vitality for us to arrange as life.

19   Peer deep into the eyes of the invisible frail,
the apathy that prevails is character burglarized.

20   Democracy is liquid freedom you drink
from the back of your hands.

21 Pedal the cycle of character,
dismiss the people of sheep,
savor the zealot they weep.

22   If you submit your soul to sail your ship,
each utility unfolds unscripted.

23   Capitalism captures fame for the fortunate
and mediocrity for the marooned.

24   Those who ask of the purpose of life
have not discovered an outer meaning
for inner designs.

25   Original fantasy is the mind's vanguard
and the bard's academy of avant-garde.

26   Lips mumble words before heard
are canvas betrays of inner songbirds.

27   Inside the swagger of your dreams
is the staggered fulcrum of esteems.

28   Stylish societies are salty satisfaction
of shifting imperfections.

29   The dogma of your dreams
is the demon of your doctrine.

30   The vaulting of emotional virtues
is the matron's design of your maze.

*31   Your life beam is to become YOUR dreams,
into the prudence of less travelled esteems.*

*32   The sparkling glitter of advanced alien thought
impairs our vital judgment when sought.*

*33   Now that I finally found myself, I desperately
miss the search for meaning.*

Retirement Quotes

*1   Retirement is a self-defining moment of karma
unfrozen.*

*2   Old age is crimson leaves of your soul
gliding softly on the timeless edges of eternity.*

*3   Growing old is graceful decode as fugitives of
time and happiness evolve at crossroads.*

*4   To be enlightened by age, take heed to enshrine
the miracle people who were designed by time.*

*5   The average person lives in numb repetition in
their small world of idleness. Yet, are amazed
how fast life has passed.*

*6   Never delay your life review, you'll need time
to complete and thank your circles of salvation.*

*7   Retirement opens the alter ego to free expression,
if you can unshackle the task of conformity.*

*8   In retirement, social age is abandoned
and you become the course of time.*

*9   Our plan for vital involvement when aging
is to discover, implement, and reap the rewards of
the social application of our passions.*

*10   The retirement diet is a salad of mixed means,
sweet please, Swiss cards, bell clever, and call
ye flowers with dreams of a thousand islands.*

*11   Your retirement identity is of a successful person
who creatively and efficiently manages your money
and
lifestyle to adapt to the ever changing economic and
personal conditions of the time.*

*12   To volunteer the heart is a springboard
of purpose in a journey of redemption.*

*13   With the curiosity of nostalgia to tout, your
ancestry is an adventurer's journey of truth and
doubt.*

*14   For your second act to abide and accrue,
you must upset your internal guru.*

*15   Retirement dating is like chasing streetcars,
a parody of character to catch as memoirs*

16   Let your second act ignite an idle mind
and pasture old habits of patterned times.

17   The folly with frail friends of strife
is vacating into victims of their own device.

18   Seize the light of gray with tributes to family and
friends, purpose lingering passions as legacy's
fashion to send.

19   Life review is an unconscious need to
close bonds of salvation as your final rhapsody.

20   There is no coffin to fear since your soul lives
beyond and travels until your future spawns.

21   All the laughs and fears and loves and tears
are measured away in yardstick years.

22   The art of aging is based on your acceptance
of the inevitable and amnesia of the measurable.

23   When your obscure your natural age,
you obscure your natural outcomes.

24   Retirement is discovering an inner light
beyond the envy of self esteem.

25   The elder mind is a tool for a limitless heart
molding a sense of loss into a carve of art.

26   Don't let phantom fear of the unknown
compose the cryptic core of your home.

*27   Adaptive aging is when your mind grills like a
gourmet despite the body baking away.*

*28   Your dwindling life expectancy is your social
calendar of meaning for an existential bucket list.*

*29   Let your legacy outshine
the soul of your meaning enshrined.*

*30   If your induce your world to shrink so small,
imagination can change the swell to sprawl.*

*31   To leave a lasting legacy on memory's shelf,
expand the unique extremes of yourself.*

*32   The questions that regret your retirement
are the demons of unfinished business.*

*33   If you prepay to send flowers after you pass,
your legacy of love lives beyond forecast.*

*34   In retirement, never let digital dances replace
the natural contact for social swagger.*

*35   Since life spans are so fragile and fleeting,
morsels of meaning seduce repeating.*

*36   When muddling in the mire of memories,
its your evolution that vaults life's tone.*

*37   Your retirement alter ego wants to build
a final identity accumulated from the fulfillment
of subconscious traits.*

Chapter 12: Children's Poems

Children's poems are supposed to be short, funny and rhyme. That's a good formula, but I find it limiting. So, I added the element of imagination or fantasy. I find the ability of children to think autonomous from structured and linear thought to be the exact foundation for creative ideas and poetry. The first two poems have previously been published.

Mr. Ben

I only have one friend
It's a little bug
His name is Mr. Ben
But, he's too small to hug

I take him to school
Tightly in a little jar
To show the kids he's cool
So I can be a star

I bring him out to play
The kids all gather to see
Some run away
While others share my glee

I'm so proud today
The teacher saw Mr. Ben
He smiled and said, okay
Now I have more friends

My Funny Cat

I know a funny cat
Who walks on my face
Early in the morning
Waking me with grace

She leaps from tall buildings
And always lands on feet
Can walk many miles home
If lost on the street

She meows only with humans
When its time to play
She sweats only through paws
When chasing her prey

She always gives me love
And often wants to chat
She's my heart's purring star
I know a funny cat

Sideways Walk

When I was a small child
I lived near a shinny bay
Where sea life runs wild
But water too cold for play

I get a hook and string
Add a little fish as bait
I drop it in the ocean
And started fishing at eight

My line moves with a swish
I pull with all my powers
It's a crab, not a fish
It took me four hours

It's orange and has ten legs
With a sideways walk
So I took it home to mom
Who cooked him in a pot

Friendly Star

Bright and rising star
Smiles of a friendly sun
A million miles too far
It's why life begun

It spins and circles we know
So it makes day and night
It pushes plants to grow
And tickles our mood delight

It gives us vitamin D
To color our bones so strong
The sun improves our sleep
Turning the body's clock on

But, don't sunbath too long
Always pocket your eyes
Too much sun is wrong
According to the wise

My Toys

My toys are special friends
They always wait for me
Until the school day ends

I name them all, of course
I talk to my little men
And ride my flower horse

I play my musical toys
As loud as I can
To dance with pretty noise

I'll color a laughing sky
I see the world through crayons
And peacocks flying by

But, when the day ends
I hug my colorful toys
And love my special friends

If I Could Fly

If only I could fly
My arms are wings of a bird
I'd travel to different countries
Where people of color are heard

I would stop in Asia
Where most of the world lives
I'd hug a giant panda
And feed a giraffe olives

I would fly to Africa
To ride a stripped zebra
Take photos of colorful animals
And run with speeding cheetahs

Then it's off to Europe
A gift for a curious eye
I'd see all the art museums
If only I could fly

Books

Books open the night sky
To moon and bright stars
To see the colorful planets
Beautiful worlds too far

Books are a magic trip
For sailing the oceans blue
I am the captain on my ship
So, I brought a zoo

Books are singing facts
And help with your math
They can tickle you with jokes
In case you want to laugh

Books are my best friends
They're full of ideas and fun
They always keep me company
And make me the smartest one

Growing Up

I can't wait to grow up
Its fun to be a kid
But, I want to reach the cookies
Way up where they're hid

I want the training wheels
Taken off my bike
I want my rolled up pants
To be straight as I like

I dream of driving a car
And watching all cartoons
To travel with friends real far
So we can follow the moon

Of course, I'll go to college
To be stylish and smart
To make Mom and Dad proud
And set myself apart

Falling Leaves

The big oak leaves are falling
At this chilly time of year
Floating so softly to earth
A mood of colorful cheer

A carpet of golden stars
Trimmed with green and red
Covering the parked cars
And blown about my head

Daylight is getting shorter
Summer has slipped away
The birds have moved south
Its sweaters and hats today

A cup of hot chocolate
Safe and warm classroom
I'll play will all my friends
While the falling season blooms

The Art of Food

When I sit down to eat
I see rainbows on my plate
Yellow corn and red meat
Asking me to create

When I have a pizza
I change all the parts
I make pepperoni zebras
And a ball of cheese for hearts

When I have long noodles
I put them on my head
And I love apple strudel
On top of my cornbread

Food is wonderful art
That I paint with my outlook
Add recipes that are smart
To put in my cookbook

My Old House

When I was a little kid
I lived in a squeaky old house
With three stories and many rooms
There once lived a little mouse

I'd see him now and then
Racing through the cracks
I'd leave him bread crumbs
And some cool aid for a snack

I followed him one night
Up and up to the highest door
He ran into its curvy crack
On the ceiling floor

I got my dad's ladder
To peek in this dusty room
Over by the window
Was a girl with a broken broom

I Love to Pretend

I love to play pretend
To become a flying car
When I'm on the school yard
To travel to the stars

I'll go to Disneyland
To meet Buzz and Snow White
I'd dance in a pirate's party
And watch the light show at night

I'd ride the biggest roller coaster
That I could possibly find
I'll wander into a small world
And shrink inside my mind

To eat hot dogs and cotton candy
With my buddy Peter Pan
I'll climb splash mountain
With my swinging dad Tarzan

Christmas Lights

Places I go are covered with snow
Others are just breezy and wet
When bones are chilly I always know
Winter brings Christmas yet

Long lines for Saint Nick at the mall
Short times for daylight to stay
Little girls wishing for a pretty doll
Bouncing boys just thrilled to play

Strings and strings of beautiful lights
Sparks glitter in every doorway
I wander around till past midnight
Hoping to meet Santa midway

I dream to travel in his sleigh
To dance with his elves at the pole
I'll hug and thank them all today
And help with his holiday goal

Ghirardelli Chocolate

Heavenly chocolate created
Aged and true and refined
Dreams of appetite elated
A favorite of all mankind

Seeking the purest that exist
In creative hands of gourmets
There is never a waiting list
To dance the desserts ballet

Delight in the circus of flavors
Originally made on site
Add fruit and ice cream to savor
Milk or dark or white

Lunch and supper take a pass
To honor the hungry child within
For chocolate wonders unsurpassed
Priority takes a mental grin

From caramel fudge sundaes
To banana splits galore
Wonders of desserts amaze
To capture my heart's amour

Best Friends

I'm your sunshine in the morning
I'm the frosting on your cake
I'm the jam on your toast
And the sizzle in your steak

You're the ham on my sandwich
You're the flavor in my tea
You're the sugar in my cookies
And the lock to my key

I'm the bounce in your step
I'm the smile in your eyes
I'm the laughter on your face
And the tears when you cry

You're the motion in my movement
You're the sharp to my smart
You're the wonder in my thoughts
And the beat of my heart

Chapter 13: Future of Society

Imagine if we had a crystal ball to see into the future. Remnants of evidence are all around us if one cares to examine. A detective pieces together oddly shaped clues to form a coherent whole of the past. An existentialist pieces clues to anticipate the coherence of the future. I naturally anticipate the future because I have this odd sense of continual time lines. Nothing begins or ends, it just continues or evolves.

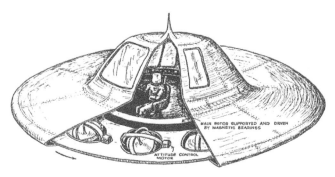

MARK II FLYING SAUCER

ELECTRONIC CENTRIFUGES BASED ON THE VORTEX DRIVE ARE MOUNTED IN GIMBALS TO TURN IN SYNCH WITH THE REVOLUTIONS OF THE MAIN ROTOR DISC.
THE TUNED ELECTROMAGNETIC FIELD GENERATED BY THE VORTEX DRIVE CAUSES THE VEHICLE TO BE CARRIED BY THE EARTH'S ELECTROMAGNETIC FIELD LIKE A DIRIGIBLE ELECTRON.
CONTROLLED GEOMAGNETIC PROPULSION IMPROVES THE DESIGN EFFICIENCY TO THE MARK III STAGE.

Get comfy in the saucer and lets take a ride into our destiny.

*The next stage of human evolution, the genetic age,
will restructure all life forms forever.*

Digital Destiny

Life is a cell phone
On automatic dial
Language is a tombstone
Ideas are a smile

Social media popular
Digital friends are sought
Become a cyber star
Society of virtual thought

My car to drive itself
I'm free to inebriate
Protection from ourselves
Safety's new blind date

Medical microchip
Embedded under my skin
To scope inside my ship
Determining next of kin

Evolving technology
Redesigning my life
Survival has lost biology
With my computer wife

Amazing maid and cook
She never acts with spite
Attractive shiny look
In libido's moonlight

Moon Memoirs

Remember the romantic moon
Sweet life and love were swooned
Reflections of whimsy and wonder
Disguised the umbrella we're under

Remember the lessons of time
When Aristotle inked his rhymes
Before the moon existed he claimed
And confirmed in the bible's frame

Remember the lunar landings
A human harvest of understanding
Until the residing grey creatures
Levied the lead as astral Caesars

To romancing the moon as old memoir
And accepting the proof as new bizarre

*No one wants to accept the studies proving the moon is a
satellite made of metal that houses a city of little grays.
Once people get over their fear of advanced creatures,
they'll be our mentors.*

Change of History

Darwin's chronology he couldn't quite connect
Huge gaps in biology of a fragmented architect

His fossil history chain is romance without a kiss
Mutations can't explain the stages sorely missed

Pyramid waves of rhythms so astrologically aligned
Built for electro magnetism to mobilize mankind

Experts stumped and scour this ancient energy plant
Renewable internal powers by ancestors of
transplants

Humans lodged alien gods, Ezekiel's account is clear
Descending in shiny pods, coexistence without fear

Elongated skulls expound the facts of mystery
Sumerian science astounds the change of history

So, we rewrite the frontiers of prior knowledge
And reform the careers of those with college

An awakening

My Crystal Ball

I can factor into the future
And become the course of time
My age has been suspended
Dark matter has shifted my mind

We'll entertain friends and foes
Who travel from other worlds
With agendas of varied audacity
Under their spell we're whirled

Language is a passing phase
Voices are a vaulted tombstone
We'll develop a higher cortex
So telepathy can tender its tone

We'll soar in flying saucers
From broken pieces we chase
We reverse engineer the debris
With electromagnetic embrace

Our talent will be time travel
To scout and sever space
Worm holes and astral portals
A dimension of time's birthplace

Most disturbing of all
We'll evolve to a hybrid race
Our DNA will be enhanced
Our characters will be replaced

The Cell Society

Waiting and waiting for words to appear
Pending and bending is a life to cohere

Texting and texting all through the day
Hoping and choking my fans don't decay

My self-esteem volleys on volume of "likes"
My friendships are frayed on emotional strikes

My babble buddies are airways that bounce
Of virtual value too costumed to count

I farewell all minds that feel of ordeal
And bodily contacts that feel of cold steel

Digital icons are top future replacements
For old relationships of tumor amazements

Congratulate me now for I'm engaged
I look forward to love in a virtual maze

Political Face

We know the political process
Has a self-defeating core
When one party blindly reverses
Progress of those before

Gullible voters abide
Who swallow all the lies
Yields them deeply unqualified
To hire a sheep's disguise

To survive self-destruction
Adversaries must archive
Cohesive solutions are the future
Digital answers have arrived

Monitor and mend social need
Programs of human montage
Tears of chaos to bias free
To finally maroon the mirage

*It is time to use a program that addresses human
needs and picks qualified applicants to elect
rather than rely on the unscrupulous.*

Feminine Zen

Womb of all societies
Gift of engendering life
Backbone to the family
Rigorous dedicated wife

Yet, history is dangling dark
Long shadows of caveman
Machismo is so dominant
Gatekeepers of life spans

Genetic horizons in question
Complex society demands
Scholarly power revolves
Esteem of bright expands

Remodel to pride of parity
Future's pristine mandate
Adaptability's new bride
Male bubbles will deflate

Male backlash of anxiety
Short circuits men of brawn
To emerge a better creature
Sophistication yet to spawn

Future regimes built by women
With brutality and crime defaced
Humanity becomes what's natural
And the art of equality embraced

Crop Circles

Geometric daring designs
  Beyond nine thousand world wide
    Rebellious rings and cagey circles
    Overlap and intersect with pride

      Stars within stars are the universe
      A double helix is our genetic house
        With circular patterns of Stonehenge
        They sketched us like a spouse

        It's the art of surgical precision
          Mysterious wisdom to unwind
          Lavished in the lyrics of science
        And musical scales aligned

      The usual government lies
     Yet radiation rages the soil
    Magnetic tools misbehave
    That ripples their blood to boil

A puzzle of cognitive design
They're still awaiting our response
Science is too cowardly and confused
To revel in this knowledge renaissance

The Next Life

I envy the afterlife
Freedom's gourmet of style
Passing through time engaged
Where reincarnation smiles

Erasing the resolve of a rebel
I'll gather my lessons of yore
 To become energy photons
Accumulated from lives before

The vogue is this grand voyage
Wisdom's universal history
To discern our primitive traits
And the origins of our mystery

Obscured from earthly sight
Where only thoughts can bode
You'll keep your personality
In a dimension that's bestowed

Woven into fabric of souls
To swim in heavenly seas
Love and peace are pristine
Your eternal harmony

To the earth, I say goodbye
Thank you for life and rhyme
Happily enshrined as alumni
To live in the crossroads of time

Pyramids

Architecture of simplicity
Magnetic funnel of earth
Invisible synchronicity
Energy for cells to rebirth

Cosmic synergies converge
Unveiling the mystery key
Healing vibrations diverge
My melanoma to debris

Harmonic copper pyramid
A mind for meditation
Electrical currency grid
The heat of new carnation

Invading with a calmness
That flows inside my veins
Thoughts and sight gain boldness
As unfolding new domains

To vanish aches and pains
Obscured in a hidden crust
Deleted in my membranes
Robust of strength from rust

Alignment of many angles
Relics of the fountain of health
To heal the body's mangles
In planetary ancestors' wealth

New World Order

Wake up call dynamo, aliens inside earth
For longer than we know, inhabiting to rebirth

Dentures of denial, dark government's way
Live evidence is viral, reptilians and little grays

Transport is magnetic exceeding speeds of light
Travel through dimensions while aging is hindsight

Many alien species rushing to drink the earth
We are discovered news of the universe

To gain technology, we granted them free reign
Dire agenda revealed, we're dancing with butane

Misjudged their intent of breeding a hybrid race
Control for the planet or humanity loosing its place

They seek an earthly abode and a new world order
A threat we must decode to freedom's divine borders

The Sweet Here After

Grapevine of departed, heartburn of returned
A date with destiny for an epoch yet earned

Reawaken in a quake, heats your inner core
Construed with a purpose novel from before

Your fate has fallout, if you scheme and shake
Your soul pays a toll if you slither like a snake

Details of life review, charming to finesse
Dark skeleton secrets are burning to confess

Meaning of your afterlife, pending on a chance
Resolving prior strife is your pivot circumstance

Journeys of philanthropy, passages so keen
Esteem of personality is your shepherd to redeem

This is from reading personal accounts of
those who passed and returned.

The Genetic Age

A ballet with biology
And rhyming with time
Fusing these elements
In a genetic paradigm

Cloning of sheep
Would you like a twin
We're beyond the beginning
Of constructing our kin

Childbirth is obsolete
Just duplicate yourself
Love and matrimony
Dusty books on the shelf

Purge parental genes
Drag the DNA strand
Defy chronic disease
Health's new rock band

Doctors will resist
Profit from illness and pain
Misinformation twist
Clouds on fortune's reign

Extract the gene of age
Live four hundred years
Shift nature into neutral
Goodbye floundering peers

Anatomy of slow motion
Revelations are profound
Genesis of many centuries
Brings hearing to ultra sound

Dream of a sage society
Longevity is by design
Rewriting mortal rules
Fantasy's new sublime

What would God say?
It wasn't meant to be
It's completely unnatural
And restructures reality

The cusp of a new age
Divisive as far can see
The gift of wealth benefits
Sans the reward of decree

Fortune's fountain of youth
For the love of high wages
From gaming the grim reaper
To dismissing the rampages

Ethics or political power
Ideologies will collide
The privilege of extra life
Money's madness to decide

Hybrids of the Sword

To unravel the genetics of yore
Is to sneak in history's back door
Cowardly is the trait of myopic minds
Primitive is the panic of archaic kinds

Homo Sapiens from God or evolution
Hoax the reality is man's social solution
Two theories of deception centuries tall
Both imposters of history's downfall

Sumerians lived with Annunnaki rock stars
The planet Nibiru is the origin of the czars
Genetic gifts from a species derived
Confirmed by alien DNA that survived

Scientific shades have rocky facts to persuade
A higher wisdom crusades past old barricades
A bonus to evolve in our little sphere
A structure for knowledge if we cohere

Enhanced species of an early hybrid
That reset religion to idioms inbred
Theological denial is retorts of discord
We are alien hybrids of a genetic sword

*NASA finally admitted that the planet Nibiru
does orbit into our solar system every 3,600 years
as confirmed with telescopic images.*

Other Side of the Moon

High resolution
On the dark side of the moon
Surviving in the shadows
An alien cocoon

Scope of their dimensions
Ignorance we know
Sporadic probing contact
Yet, seclusive like Thoreau

Anxious we've been appraised
Their image we now access
With a style of uncertainty
They're heedless to coalesce

For the doubters of today
Morphed are minds off guard
Proof blinds your thoughts
The future's avant garde

Dimensions of a shell
Hollowed by alien design
Waive as they float by
Friends of our lunar shrine

To wander in another world
Is to bargain the risk our being
While we stumble through life
Our mind's eye never seeing

The puzzle of a protocol
For unlocking the universe
Is to swim and let stroke
In the cultures of outskirts

We can sashay to their abode
With the curiosity of a cat
We send caution to the wind
And engage their habitat

Yet, mindfulness is vital
An impulsive faux pas
Could topple our empire
Fatality's tragic flaw

Superior beyond our fears
We're urgent to be taught
Yet, why reveal their secrets
To primitive crackpots

Lock politicians whole
Bulls in a crystal shop
Arrogance and control
A disaster without a mop

Rookies to space travel
With fear of evolution
Aggressions might decide
Our stay of execution

Scholars made of thought
Judgment based on wit
Decryption is their clout
Uncanny savvy fits

Time solves this mystery
Pray for intelligent hands
Our minds could be molded
Or simply turned to sands

Chapter 14: Essays and Narratives

In these narratives and conceptual essays, I have a passionate intensity to dissect archaic ideas and turn them on their head. This was done to some extend in the poetry, but while metaphors can be freeing, structure can be limiting. Ride with me through the wormhole as we bend time and space with social commentary and future expectations.

Freedom is the liquidity of thought
while creativity is the solidity of outcomes.

Haight Ashbury 1968

Imagine yourself in an upscale area with colorful Victorian homes from a gilded era. You feel the cool alkalinity of the ocean's breeze in your face. You scan the free-and-wild-to-be people of the melting pot and developing youth culture questioning the oppressive rigors of the day. This is my origin and point of reference for understanding the universe.

It was 1968 and I was 14 years old when a school friend and I first saw the Haight Ashbury at night. The bustling streets were littered with scraggly teenagers who had run away from home without any money. There were 15 to 20 sardine panhandlers per block wearing tie-dye shirts, bell bottoms, headbands and flower necklaces. My first impression was that of horror--how could so many young people be homeless at the same time? They were mostly broke, had few belongings, and no place to sleep.

As we walked, we heard voice after voice, "Spare change, spare change." We slipped into a hippie poster shop to escape the noisy fray. These posters were glowing with bright colors despite darkness of only a violet light. I was spellbound by the fluorescent designs that covered all the walls and ceiling. I felt I was on a different planet. Floating high in the air was this wispy bouquet of an old skunk. A beautiful woman with flowers woven into her long blond hair handed me a rainbow stogie. Not wanting to look childish, I pretended I knew how to smoke.

My coughing and gagging brought down my charade so quickly that we found ourselves back out on the street allowing curiosity to drive our direction. Why did you risk coming here? I had to ask a couple of the kids. "We want to be part of the movement," I was told. They talked of the need for social change, to stop the war, to strive for peace and equality for all.

Still confused, I couldn't see how coming to the San Francisco would bring about the social change they desired. Most were runaways and hungry and just moving with the flow of pan handling, freedom seeking, and soul searching. The Haight Ashbury free clinic opened a year earlier or it would have been much worse.

The open fields of Golden Gate Park became a refuge as it was turned into a hippie campsite of optimistic visionaries. Some people were kind enough to open their homes so the kids had a place to sleep--flop houses. I decided that flopping would be the experience that would really set me free. So, I committed myself the next night. I put on my tie-dye shirt, woven headband, and some funky beads. I hid a sandwich in my backpack and headed back to Haight Street to blend into the movement.

I was taken aback when I found these hippies would advocate for those in need. If I were hungry, they would search out food for me. When I said I needed a place to sleep, they introduced me to a couple that opened their home where I stayed. I remember a wonderful vegetable stew the owners graciously made for the kids that night. I was a bit surprised to be fed and even more amazed when they asked if I was ok. I'll never forget this middle age couple that seemed to care, perhaps, they heard the growl in our stomachs or saw the fear in our faces.

There were about ten kids who were welcome to spend the night on their living room floor. As the group talked and joked, I was able to learn of their plight. It was about senseless violence, distrust for the president, repression of new ideas, pressure to conform and lack of freedoms. They had all lost confidence and faith in a government that persisted in war. They rejected being drafted to kill others for political reasons. They just wanted to peacefully determine the outcome of their own lives.

Their devoted and heartfelt willingness to sacrifice the comfort of their homes for social change had lasting impact on me. I had never seen courage or foolish risk-taking like this before. It opened up the rebel inside me that became part of my alter ego and identity. I think and interact in the world differently with this background. For that, I thank the Haight Ashbury for molding my heart and mind.

Fatherhood

The wonder of having children is one of the scariest events in life if you're a man. It's not on the early agenda or bucket list of any men I know. Then I was given the ultimatum, have a child or look for a new relationship. Wow, no shades of gray or methods of compromise. Women have a keener sense of procreation than men. I envy the resolve of fulfilling your purpose when the goal is clear in your heart and mind. I had been in this relationship for ten years and starting over seemed daunting at the time. So, I just tucked my personal uncertainty in my back pocket and hoped to build on what we already had.

Positive anticipation clearly goes a long way in these matters. I was surprised with all the stages leading up to childbirth. First, the process of trying to get pregnant is a challenge. It brought a new meaning to "that time of month." Then it's nine months of pregnancy itself with the related social rituals.

Now I'm sitting in the operating room holding mother's hand. Surrounding by no less than six medical staff and a dizzying array of technology. She can't feel anything from her waist down, so there is calmness on her face. We wait until a little foot begins to slip out. Then the legs and body, but stops at the head. A little problem quickly resolved as I take a deep breath. Up on mommy's tummy with fluid dripping and eyes closed. A new life has been created where none existed before. This amazing moment is freeze framed in my memory forever as I reach for my camera.

Cyclones of future scenarios of responsibility are spinning in my mind. I realize my life trajectory is changed by this extension of myself. It's the balance of a high wire act with two independent identities of change. I'm suddenly worried about our education system, children's health care, and a clean and safe environment like never before. My priorities adjusted to my character with the emergence of latent traits previously unknown to me.

I was pleasantly surprised that fatherhood unlocks your inner child to come out and play again. I'm so glad for my daughter that it brought out care-taking, patience and commitment that I didn't know was in me. I now feel the joy, love, confusion and pain exactly the way she does.

The intensity and loyalty of this bond took me a bit by surprise. My friends, who saw the joy of our connection, said that we're lucky to have each other. I do feel lucky, but also determined to be the best father possible. I have this enduring feeling that our souls are connected forever in the eternal world. I even have planned adventures with her in the afterlife. This is fatherhood.

The Wake Up Call

My parents broke up when I was seven years old and the family moved to a small subsidized apartment in an old and fading neighborhood. One adult and three kids with only two bedrooms meant the couch was mine. Mother, who chose not to work, was stressfully preoccupied with stretching the welfare pittance. My clothes were tattered hand me downs and my shoes were frayed and torn. People would leave bags of rice and beans at our door because they knew our situation. We were always in arrears with the rent and moved frequently when the landlords reached their tolerance level. This happened so often that we left our belongings in bags and boxes. As kids, we accepted this as simply our reality.

One evening the family came to the dinner table as usual. I watched my mother provide a slice of bread with peanut butter on it for my two sisters. She graced me the same, but when she reached in the bag for herself, there was none left. I noticed a sadness come over her face as she stared down at her empty plate. My sisters were hungry, so they ate fast and were on their way. Being a little older, I noticed what happened. I stayed to watch her clean the table and wash the dishes before leaving. She didn't say anything about this nor did she talk much the rest of the evening.

My mind was tangled with frustration and sadness. I knew this was wrong, but I felt powerless to change it. I remember searching for a solution, an option, an answer. After hours of gut churning rumination, I still felt a pain in my heart. I didn't know if I should praise my mother for feeding the kids first or blame her for putting us in this desperate situation. This continues to fester inside me for days as I sought some understanding.

Despite being only twelve, I concluded that money was the dirty culprit. What we do; where we live; who we are often depends on wealth. This is what society values, what motivates us, and what give us respect and status. The pensive days of childhood following this event changed my life. I recognized money as a surly monster needing to be tamed. Unaware of it at the time, this became my lifelong wake up call. It was the springboard of motivation into education, investing, and frugality. These values have been carved into my identity forever.

Dissecting my ancestry led me to discover a series of poverty wake up calls that were not responded to. What was this invisible dragon tormenting my ancestors rendering them unable to wake up to the call? These rare opportunities for growth and change may only grace you once in your lifetime. If you can't rise to the urgency of occasion, you may live in the shadows forever.

Computer Dating

You're dancing with your heart as you await a response from your perfect date. You just opened your diary and spilled out a long and detailed email of your personal feelings and hopes for the future as a couple. You can envision the happiness and intimacy beginning to form already. After years of searching, you now realize that you have found the "one." It has been a couple of days, but no response yet. So, you send it again, thinking it was probably a computer glitch. But, it was the loudest silence you've ever heard.

The next learning experience was a date I couldn't find. When people include photos on their dating page, a common trick is to post youthful shots of yore. So, when you met for coffee, the first challenge is to recognize them. I was shocked when it turned out she were sitting arm's distance away. I casually mentioned that their photo looks like a different time and person. "It's a few years old," I am told. It looked over 20 years old with a face of high school youth. Yet, this was the best level of integrity this person could offer.

Then there was the late dinner of Japanese cuisine for our first meeting. We knew virtually nothing of each other and were prompted only by the photos. She wore all black from head to toe that contrasted with bleach blond hair. When she spoke, it was music to my ears. The intelligence and insight flowed into me like a Mozart symphony. Our allegro lasted for hours and the united harmony endured for years.

Computer dating is like driving a car backwards. You normally meet someone you find attractive and get to know them over time. On the computer, you get to know them or their facade first and try to be attracted to them later. It may sound very beneficial to know of the extremely important character first. However, if the other person doesn't trigger your sense of attraction, they're just passing ships.

Living in the crossroads of romance and technology is like having a microchip in your heart. You avail your emotions to respond to digital prompts from strangers of unknown backgrounds with dubious intent. The cloak of anonymity allows the pretenders to flourish into new identities. Yet, they risk becoming self-defeated as soon as you meet. The irony is that a characteristic of computer dating is deception while the necessary ingredients to start a relationship are honesty and trust.

Can this impersonal, calculating, digital wave of dating really be the future for us all? Are the social circles of intermingling no longer attracting acceptable partners? If so, we all need to develop new detective skill sets. Abilities that interpret the subtle, react to the empty, and deflect the fiction. It's still possible to find a partner this way, once you learn to drive backwards.

Parallel Reality

I start my day with a metal detector and a frisk. The heavy iron door of bars squeaks its way open as I enter a transition room to wait for the next door to open. I pass through the electrical fences where I notice a bird dangling in the wind. I enter another room where I show a special pass and receive a monitor so I can be detected by computer. I wait for more doors to open.

My office is a converted prison cell with no windows, no phone and a toilet in the corner. I constantly hear the crash of the iron doors and occasional screams in the background. I grab some coffee and walk through an open yard of 300 convicted felons milling around with nothing to do. They are all big and muscular from pumping weights all day. I arrive at the administration segregation (ad. seg.) building and wait for more doors to open.

Ad. seg. is a prison within a prison. It's for inmates who commit crimes while in prison which are mostly gang fighting and stealing. Within that is another prison called "psych ad. seg." which is my focus. These are the most violent of the criminally insane and must be in cages at all times. It's time to begin my group therapy.

The inmates are placed in portable cages about the size of a telephone booth arranged in a circle so they can see each other. As I peer through the bars at them,

I ask each one to talk about their depression. An exhausted looking middle age man spoke first, "My mind is playing tricks on me cause I see things on the wall," he mumbled. "They are mostly faces of people from long ago or who died." Talk to the faces, I tell him, find out what they want and what they're feeling. Help solve their problems and make peace with them.

A young tall serious man with tattoos covering his body asked to speak. He said he was here for his own protection because he dropped out of a gang that is retaliating against him for being a traitor. You're not allowed to leave a gang unless you start a family. "So, I get locked up in isolation and they walk the yard free," he complained. "Worse yet, there's no way out of this," as he slumped lower. "Just re-join the gang," a member said, "that solves your problem." He claimed he couldn't do that since it obliges him to commit more crimes for the gang.

Your attitude is still in rebellious mode, I told him. Your first assignment is to re-set your future with a new intent and plan. It's time to be a family man even in prison. Since you only have a few years left here, begin communicating with the lonely hearts and establish a relationship. Let the gang know your intent and even be open to marriage while in prison. You need a new direction, a new life, I told him; start working on it today.

An older man with severe red and chapping skin began to speak, "I'm a lifer, but I just want to know one thing. When I feel like killing myself, what do I do?" He didn't go into detail about his thoughts or the cause, but was clearly in distress. First, I said, accept them as just passing thoughts that you don't act upon. Strip them of their value and importance. Also, start to exercise when you feel them; it helps to lower anxiety and improve mood. Re-focus your attention on something interesting or mentally demanding and don't dwell on the past. Have some absorbing goals you can always work on. I also spoke with his psychiatrist about a medication increase.

This was the first of my four groups of parallel reality for the day. I can't change their situation, but I can change how they feel about it.

Creative Rebelling

Rejecting the status quo is only the beginning of a long period of discovery. Your creative mindset is that anything can be improved upon—anything! You view expired artistic masters as simply points in time. You view past scientific breakthroughs as just one step in many. You may view yourself or the human race as a meandering ship seeking a port of answers.

To truly be creative and invent the edges of imaginations, the blank canvas of your heart seeks to be unconventional. All the great masters of the past did something unique and unusual to get where they are. Many of us can rebel in our minds to establish aspects of identity, but your heart is a different matter. I'm referring to emotional rather than intellectual rebellion.

We all have the serendipity of hidden agendas running free in our hearts. We've been told it's only a passing phase of adolescence. In truth, its purpose is always a dynamic matter of self-expression and growth. It's dynamic because growth occurs as a result of experience. So, each person has a genetic need to "be your complete self" on some level as part of the personality unfolding.

In my field of healthcare, I witnessed this rebellion develop. The American medical system is by far the most expensive while providing only an average quality of care compared to the rest of the world. The genius of this system keeps patients artificially addicted to medications while price gouging retired folks into bankruptcy. Mainstream medicine ignores natural, holistic, behavioral and preventative alternatives. Its focus is on profit by treating the symptoms of illness with drugs and surgery. As a result, doctor errors are the third leading cause of death in the U. S. ahead of car accidents. Aware of this, masses of people are rebelling that created a new industry, *medical tourism*.

In this case example of situational rebellion, personal need was the driving force. In their minds, they knew when it was time to rebel even if they hadn't rebelled before. Mental rebelling doesn't mean changing the status quo as much as it means finding a solution for you. It often takes a mass movement of a dire purpose for significant social change to occur. That means the persistence of group rebellion over time. It means joining an organization of like minds for social change and incorporating it into your lifestyle.

Rebelling for its own sake is an exercise in freedom for the novice. If your goal is change, it's less effective to rebel indiscriminately. Since we are creatures of habit, change is resisted and even feared. So, one learns the best time and manner to present contrary thought for the best reception—selective rebellion. Otherwise, you could be easily dismissed as simply defiant and your message lost.

I believe protesting is the purest form of creativity since its result is progress through awareness. So, rebellion is first motivated by a pressing personal need, satisfaction for expression, and then reinforced socially. Unless its technology, widespread change occurs only at times of social distress.

Rebelling will make you more aware of your traits, strengths, biases and how you really feel. This is part of your genetic code; its all variations of who you are that makes you whole and unique. In conclusion, I believe that creative rebelling allows your hidden passions to blossom into the character of your dreams.

Psychotherapy

It's fashionable in some circles while proof of weakness in others. Few realize that the life of a therapist is living in the shadows of others. As we seek to shed light on them, we blend into the darkness of their past. Our intent becomes fragmented into transitional emotional conflicts of their memory. Clients are marbled with particles of their therapist's traits.

When you attempt to rearrange the historical perception of others for over thirty-five years, many shades of complexity are reveled. Working in the state penitentiary system reveals more shades of misery that few witness. This is where childhood traumas set the stage for lifelong tragedy as they are unconsciously reenacted in adulthood.

Ever wonder what kind of person desires a career where you hear and feel all the pain and depression of people on a daily basis? It's one who has experienced pain or depression and who has worked to overcome it. Within this lies a hidden secret: most therapists haven't overcome personal issues enough to allow them to be effective. At least half, at all levels, are still shackled by personal demons running free.

Yet, this simple process of conversation continues to trim the branches of anxiety. Before we are therapists or clients, we are the result of our human condition. We are social beings with a capacity to care for others despite our own shortcomings. Caring, on some level, is the basis for all beneficial relationships. It is this intent and demonstration of caring that becomes the foundation for all healing regardless of the source.

Caring transcends time and place as I still care for my passed clients. I hope they find refuge no matter where they are. This type of objective caring, as I call it, can occur in many relationships. Friendships and colleagues come to mind first because family often entails emotional baggage or subjective caring. A best friend who is not judgmental has been the informal therapist of life for most people. The healing power of a deep friendship is equivalent to a good spouse that is beyond equivalent to an effective therapist.

This might seem to tilt the scale toward relying on social supports as a form of healing. But, there is a downside of turning a friend into a therapist that sometimes alters the balance into a one sided event. It's important to be sure that supportive caring flows in both directions similar to before. A therapist accepts providing care without any in return. Friends or colleagues will expect some form of reciprocity.

In conclusion, the wonder of psychotherapy is already imbedded into the social fabric of our relationships. The quality of these relationships is roughly equivalent to its healing ability. Before counseling became monetized, our therapy was from family, friends and clergy. I find that providing support to friends often triggers extended support for oneself. It's a give-and-take situation that benefits with time and effort. In conclusion, our entire social network can be made up of reliable, caring, and objective friends who don't particle your personality.

Your Bucket List

The 2007 movie The Bucket List, with Jack Nicholson and Morgan Freeman, confirmed what many people do on a more casual level. If this movie encouraged you to start your list, then you're already in transition. That is, we transition from goals based on need to goals based on meaning. Although the movie received mixed reviews, we can glean a couple of important lessons from it.

First, the movie shows how the main characters designed their bucket list at the end of their lives. Waiting until illness occurs is clearly too late to completely enjoy it. Had they never thought of completing life's dreams until they were told they would die? So, don't let the timing or fear of a bucket list delay your from realizing your dreams.

Second, the desire to go back in time to resolve an unsettled issue sometimes arises. It's not unusual to have some regrets or feel something in your past is unfinished. Perhaps, you turned down a marriage, dismissed a friendship, passed on a job offer, of feel you let your kids down in some way. If you find yourself in a position where you have a desire and opportunity to resolve something in the past, then it may be closure you're seeking.

I recently was able to gain closure on bucket item that I didn't know I needed for many years. I lived in Seattle when I was eight years old and had dreams of riding the monorail and dining in the space needle.

These dreams were nearly forgotten when I moved away and got involved with the demands of making a living. In retirement, its common to do a life review and discover unfinished business. These old dreams were awakened and the need to complete this circle of life resurrected. It was over 50 years later that I returned to the place of childhood memories. I was amazed at the details still in my head and it was absolutely exhilarating to have closure. It feels like a piece of your life has finally been completed as if you just finished a lost painting.

Third, the other confirmation from the movie and from my experience is that sharing your bucket list with someone, and participating in the activities of other peoples' bucket lists, increases your enjoyment. I encourage you to involve others as much as possible to make your experience socially and emotionally richer. A typical bucket list has different goals with different people. I took my daughter to Seattle and found that sharing this memory created a deeper bond.

Of course, its common that most of us do things with specific people depending on their interests and background. It's appropriate to take this into account when identifying the right friends or family to pair with the right event. You may find that your friends or family included you in a bucket item. Sharing your ideas with others who are actively pursuing their own goals is exciting and thought expanding. I'm in the process now of attempting to coordinate the bucket goals of my retired friends. There is nothing more fun than a group of bucket adventurers out to have a great time.

Fourth, it desensitizes and resets your attitude in dealing with end-of-life issues. That is, the more you are expose to the unknown the more comfortable your become. Some people take photos of their completed adventures and organize them into bucket albums so they can revisit their dream. I can personally attest to the fact that completing any bucket list is exhilarating, will give you a sense of completion, and will make you feel more connected to yourself and the world.

Never underestimate the impact that a bucket list has on your self-esteem and sense of well being. The connection and closure you achieve turns out to be one of the most profound of your life. Returning to the past creates a cohesive timeline for your present identity. The social part of your bucket list forges new meaning previously overlooked. Most important, you complete your dreams and ready yourself to the future.

Artificial Consciousness

Living in the digital age certainly has its advantages. Computers have infiltrated and unwittingly changed most areas of our lives. We have seen significant improvements in our homes, transportation, agriculture, defense, business, medicines and even procreation as in test tube babies. The field of Artificial Intelligence (AI) or abilities exhibited by machines, is moving forward into an area called Artificial Consciousness(AC). This is where a responsive learning is engineered into the software.

As AI has progressed over the years, machines have been programmed to learn. This developed out of pattern recognition and algorithms. It can make predictions based on collected data integrated into these patterns. This mathematical based program can find abnormalities in the patterns and make decision accordingly. Programming and learning have blurry lines in this model.

The concept of a machine consciousness with alertness, judgment, subjectivity and unique responsiveness is still far away depending when you're reading this. Progress has been rapid and accelerating. The goal is to get a learning robot in every home and replace human labor.

A second goal is to reincarnate dead people with a cyborg type machine. Take for example if your child dies prematurely. You have a computer download all her thoughts and experiences, make a physical copy, and your daughter has come back to cyborg life. But, is this the future we all want?

Computer parts embedded into our bodies since 1958, the first cardiac pacemaker, have already enhanced us. Since that time, computer chips have been installed for various reasons as a form of record keeping to spinal chip implants for pain relief. The public is aware of the benefits and accepts this invasion as long as it helps. The logical next step is a chip in the brain to enhance cognitive functions--to stimulate our intelligence.

Accepting computer parts in our bodies is a far cry from accepting cyborg robots. This brings up the fundamental question of whether we want to interact with robots instead of people? We are only willing to accept robots as enhancers. I know this because a study was done to replace psychotherapists with a software model. You tell your problems to the machine and the responses are based on patterns of others. The patients who tried this all hated it and claimed it would never replace humans.

So, we really don't want to replace humans with machines, but we are willing to accept robots for certain purposes and implants if beneficial. The second debate is that we don't want a machine doing all our activities. Many of us find great purpose, meaning, and enjoyment in our work and want to continue it. We don't want to become second-class citizens to a machine. Therefore, I believe the AI or AC robots will be limited in scope rather than control all systems

If you're really curious the future, just take a look at the alien technology we have seen so far. When spaceships crash, we found the dead aliens, but no robots. Sure, there are computers throughout and high tech weapons like flash guns. Instead, the aliens have found ways to enhance their mental skills with advanced powers. We know they speak to each other telepathically which humans have yet to develop and something computers can't do. Advanced civilizations have already been through these digital growing pains.

In conclusion, despite the momentum and fascination of AI and AC, the human aspect is being ignored. Some scientists feel that full implementation of AC would be the end of the human race. People will always want to bond with other people and have families while few, if any, will accept cyborg replacements. I think the entire AI and AC focus is based on a misunderstanding of the human mind. The human mind wants to advance, not be replaced

The DNA of Religion

The latest news of recovered blood samples of Jesus have been submitted for DNA analysis. Scientists are not disputing the correctness of the sample since it was confirmed. The results are in and we are all surprised, they claim. It turns out his DNA is only half human. His mother had the normal 23 chromosomes while his father had only one. This makes Jesus the first **scientifically confirmed** hybrid of the human race.

Many of you may know about Ezekiel's account in the Bible of a craft coming down from the heavens. He mentions that it was metal, had moving wheels, and was very bright with fire and lights. He saw four images levitate down from the ship. He interprets this as angels at the time since his only framework is religion in 600 B.C. This is confirmed in the Book of

Enoch where Enoch details a spaceship that took him aboard that he called a "fiery chariot." In the 4th century A.D., he discusses how this chariot "ascended to heaven." These accounts of the Gods coming down in vehicles are littered throughout history in many different cultures and times.

I have great respect for both religion and science and feel they will refine each other. As they intermingle, our foundations of faith will be questioned, doubted, and debated. This pesky pursuit of truth through science goes beyond how we feel about religion. It's about our very origins, our nature as humans, and our historical relationship with interplanetary beings. This discovery changes world history and our biological definition.

I have no motivation to "prove" anything to you since the evidence has already caused a stir in many circles. I prefer to objectively respond to the facts and anticipate social reactions. The Ezekiel verse has been overlooked or re-interpreted by clergy for centuries. If he really saw God, why would he need a metal ship like an alien? Some clergy fear that acknowledging information like this will topple their industry. It wouldn't be the first time that science or technology disrupted an entire industry with something new.

The current DNA results seem to confirm what Ezekiel and others witnessed long ago. Primitive man was so amazed and perplexed with these events that they surrendered their hearts and minds to them. They were so impressed with the advanced powers of alien technology; they thought they must be Gods. Our advantage in the modern era is that we have seen dead and live aliens and have their DNA. Advanced alien technology explains the miracles of Jesus including the levitation Ezekiel discussed. We know they have antigravity technology and are helping us develop it. We simply have more knowledge and experience now to make a better assessment and gain a more accurate understanding. What will the fallout of all this be? Of course, there will be extreme resistance as with any paradigm changing discovery. Clergy has already said that the presence of non-human DNA is proof of God.

But, that sounds like an oxymoron to me. Despite the long and deeply cultural nature of religion, you can sense change in the air. A solution is that the church could revise its faith to focus on social philanthropy, the soul, and the afterlife. Perhaps this is a bigger concern than proving the genetics of Jesus anyway. We now have evidence of part of the soul's path by all the near death experience reports. The church could embrace this, but that would take a leap of facts.

Human nature being what it is, I don't expect the church to revise their theology. This is the only institution I know that doesn't update with the changing times or research and is still in existence. Holding on to the past, true or not, gives many a sense of continuity and security. However, as new factual discoveries are reported and debated, it's also human nature that doubt and even distrust will grow.

As a species, we are in the process of learning and changing and will evolve in the direction of fact based thought, not dogma. As with any institution that serves people, you must evolve with the needs of your clientele or risk becoming obsolete. In conclusion, I'm afraid to say that the church's days appear numbered as they increasingly lose credibility. It will take time, but I expect that humans will outgrow a need for superstition. We will look back one day and cherish religion as a relic of the social rituals of the times.

See you in the next dimension

INDEX